Dover M
Gardner-Webb University
P.O. Box 836
Boiling Springs, N.C. 28017

Arousing the Sleeping Giant

Arousing the Sleeping Giant

How to Organize Your Church for Action

ROBERT K. HUDNUT

HARPER & ROW, PUBLISHERS

New York, Evanston, San Francisco, London

BV
652
.H75
1973

FIRST EDITION

Library of Congress Cataloging in Publication Data

Hudnut, Robert K
   Arousing the sleeping giant.
   Includes bibliographical references.
   1. Church management. I. Title.
BV652.H75   254   73–6334
ISBN 0–06–064064–2

To the beloved community
Who are St. Luke Presbyterian Church
Wayzata, Minnesota

Men hit only what they aim at.

Thoreau

If this plan . . . is of men, it will fail;
but if it is of God, you will not be able
to overthrow them.

Acts 5:38–39

Contents

Preface   xi
1 How to Become an Organizer   1
2 How to Plan   10
3 How to Write a Plan for Your Church   19
4 The Church as Suffering Servant   27
5 The Church Studies   38
6 The Church Shares   46
7 The Church Serves   58
8 How to Answer Objections to Planning   76
9 How to Organize Your Minister   84
10 How to Keep Your Minister Organized   96
11 How to Introduce the Plan to Your Church   110
12 How to Sell the Plan to Your Church   115
13 How to Organize the Money   120
14 How to Keep Your Church Organized   124
15 How to Be Organized by the Spirit   132
Appendices
  1 Letters and Comments Con and Pro   145
  2 Official Board Minutes   171
  3 The Consultation on Church Union (COCU)   177
Notes   184

Preface

This book is for anyone who wants to organize his or her church for action. If you don't want to get down to the nitty gritty, then don't read this book. On the other hand, if you, lay person or clergy, want to see your church at last *count* for something in your community, this may be the book you've been looking for.

It is a follow-up to *The Sleeping Giant: Arousing Church Power in America,* published by Harper & Row in 1971. In the *Giant* I adduced statistical and other evidence to demonstrate that the church in America in the 1970s is in sad shape, that it creates less of a stir in the press than the orange-juice ads, and that one way to whip it into shape is to *tell* everyone that certain things, going back to the first church, are *expected* of them as church members. If they don't like the expectations, then they need not join the church. If they're in and not measuring up, they can measure up or get out.

Now all that may be very fine, of course, but how do you *do* it? What is the program, what is the *plan,* for implementing these conditions of membership in *your* church at the corner of State and Main? This book was written in response to those questions. It is, in effect, a local-action handbook to *The Sleeping Giant.*

It was also written in response to an invitation from President

James I. McCord of Princeton Theological Seminary, Princeton, New Jersey, to deliver the second week's convocation lectures at the 1972 Princeton Institute of Theology.

I hold no brief for this plan's being the best or the only. But I *do* hold a brief for planning to be done by local churches. Naturally, I think the plan we have used at St. Luke Presbyterian Church in suburban Minneapolis is good. It certainly shows where we have failed. But the main thing is that the congregation *must* plan. It must plan now. And the plan must have bite. Otherwise the church as we know it is not going to make it out of the 1970s. Which may, of course, be just what is needed.

Arousing the Sleeping Giant

ONE

How to Become an Organizer

It's all very simple, just like anything else. If you want to organize your church for action, it has to become an *issue* for you. If it isn't an issue, forget it. If you think it might be, keep reading.

There are some very simple rules you must follow if you want to organize your church for action.

Rule #1.   **Get mad.**

If you're not really worked up about something, you won't be able to organize your way out of a paper bag.

Rule #2.   **Stay mad.**

Plenty of people get mad. But then they get over it on the golf course. Only the people who *stay* mad can organize.

Rule #3.   **Lose sleep over it.**

If it doesn't keep you awake at night, you don't have an issue. More to the point, the issue doesn't have you.

Rule #4.   **Lose your appetite over it.**

If you can't feel it in your stomach, forget it. You're not mad enough.

Rule #5.   **Think about it at work.**

If it doesn't take your mind off your job occasionally, it's not an issue. It is obviously not bothering you enough.

Rule #6.   **Think about it on your weekends.**

If it doesn't interrupt your scuba diving, you don't have an issue. You may have a cause, but you don't have an issue. Plenty of people have causes; only organizers have issues. One person with an issue is worth a congregation with a cause.

Rule #7.   **Get one other person.**

Rule #8.   **Each of you get another.**

Rule #9.   **Each get another.**

You now have 8. If you do this 10 more times you will have 8,192.

Rule #10. **Write a plan.**

Yes, write it. In three parts.
1. *What* we want to do.
2. *How* we want to do it.
3. *Who's* going to do *what, when.*

Rule #11. **Work your plan.**

Keep everyone accountable. Have regular report-backs to the entire group—not just to you. If a person hasn't done his job, he's got to say it to the group. Volunteers have to be embarrassed into action.

Rule #12. **Count on your opposition.**

They'll come through for you every time.

Rule #13. **Don't worry about defections.**

Even Jesus, a genius at organizing, lost 1/12 of his group. That's almost 10%. At the end, he had lost them all.

Rule #14. **Have fun with your tactics.**

If it isn't fun, don't do it.

Rule #15. **Keep your tactics simple.**

If the first person you meet on the street cannot understand instantly what you are doing, don't do it. Go back to the drawing board. Obviously you have not planned enough.

Rule #16. **Keep your people involved.**

If you can't, you're not an organizer. This means getting them in on the planning. People like to be consulted. If they're in early they'll stay late. Flatter them that you want their ideas. You do. In the organizing game, nobody has all the answers.

Rule #17. **Keep your paperwork down.**

If you have to write it out for people, you're dead. More revolutions are killed by the mimeograph than anything else. If it isn't simple enough so you can explain it in 60 seconds to a 10-year-old, you don't have an issue. Tactics are beside the point. Go back to the drawing board.

Rule #18. **Revise your plan.**

You *must* write one thing. And that is your plan for your hard core of 8. Keep it up to date. Constantly revise it. Your target may have shifted. Your tactics may have become obsolete. This could happen *any time*. It does. Keep alert.

Rule #19.   **Have a thick skin.**

> "If you can't take the heat," Truman said, "stay out of the kitchen." If you can't take hostility, stay out of organizing. Whenever you tamper with the status quo, you are bound to make enemies. Welcome them. They prove that your tactics are being successful.

Rule #20.   **Put down your Bible.**

> Take it up, yes, but know when to put it down. There are two types of people, the readers and the organizers. Organizers know when to stop research and start action. Most people feel they can't move until they have all the facts. But since they will never have all the facts they will never move. It is one of the great copouts of all time. Stop reading and start organizing.

Rule #21.   **Don't get caught in the ends-means bag.**

> "I agree with your ends," your "friends" will tell you, "but I disagree with your means." It's a classic copout. Everybody chooses means appropriate to his end. It's going on all the time in the corporation, the school, the church, the home, the government. "No axiom is more clearly established in law or in reason," Madison wrote in *Federalist Paper 44,* "than that wherever the end is required, the means are authorized."

Rule #22. **Remember that your weakness is your strength.**

> You are *not* an expert at organizing. That is your strength. You are a plain, average, ordinary Christian doing a plain, average, ordinary Christian thing, organizing people to become a church. If the old way of leaving it to the "experts" in business, government, and church had worked, that would be one thing. But it hasn't. That's why you're organizing. "Everyone says I'm politically naive," says Joan Baez, "and I am. But so are the people running politics, or we wouldn't be in wars, would we?"

Rule #23. **Get discouraged.**

> It's healthy. If you had nothing to be discouraged about, you wouldn't be in the organizing game in the first place. It would all *be* organized and you wouldn't have anything to do.

Rule #24. **Keep the faith.**

> Your church *can* be made to work. All it takes is organization. The system is dehumanized because people have not organized to humanize it. *You* are an organizer because you believe the church *can* "turn the world upside down" (Acts 17:6). That's what the Christian dream is all about.

*

This is simply another way of saying, if you want to organize your church for action, wait for the Spriit.

That sounds pious. It is. There is nothing wrong with piety. The word is not a pejorative. It evokes an essential quality of life.

If you want to organize your church because you want to "get the minister," or because you want to be a "successful minister," or because you want more money given to the candelabra, or because you want some way to get your extracurricular kicks, then you have no business trying to organize your church. All you're doing is organizing your own hangups. And there's no reason why 300 or 3,000 other people should have to be in on that.

"Wait on the Lord." Pray about it. Is this your thing? Will you have the stamina? The discipline? It will take a minimum of 5 hours a week for a year.

But don't wait forever. "God will do the planning" is another classic copout in churches. A man fixed up the vacant lot next door. "My, what a good job you and God have done," his friend said. "Yeah," he replied, "but you should have seen it when God had it all to himself."

However, there is one warning. For every 100 people who want to organize their church, only 10 should and only 1 will. That's fine. It is exactly the way it should be. The Spirit does the winnowing. If it didn't, there would be chaos.

Of course, there are many who argue that chaos is what we need. It is the only way to correct an excessive amount of "order." The analogy is drawn to the American Revolution.

I don't buy that. The system is too good. There is more democracy in the local church than there is in the local government. The vote is given to 14-year-olds. There are annual elections, frequent meetings, what amounts to initiative, referendum, and recall by virtually any member. Anyone can speak. All meetings are open.

*

It is obvious, then, that the whole organizing game is what you feel in your gut. If you feel deeply about organizing your church for action, you will. If you don't, you won't. It's just that simple.

The tragedy is that we have too few people who really feel that their church *needs* to be organized for action. Either they delude themselves into thinking their church *is* organized. Or they salve themselves into thinking that it *should* be organized, but that it's not their thing. After all, they put in 40 hours a week on the job, and that's about max for hard work, which is what organizing is.

Nevertheless, because you have read this far, *you* are among the 10 who should be organizing *your* church, at the corner of State and Main, for action. Welcome, and keep reading.

*

Check list to see if your church *needs* to be organized for action. If you answer No to any of the questions, your church *does* need to be organized. If you answer No to more than ½ the questions, you'd better fire your minister. If you answer No to all the questions, you'd better dissolve your church and begin over.

1. Does your church give a dollar to others for every dollar it spends on itself?
2. Are 1/3 of your church's Sunday school teachers adult men, 1/3 adult women, and 1/3 youth?
3. Are more than 1/3 of the youth "active"?
4. Are you losing at least 10% of your membership a year?
5. Is your budget growing at least 10% a year?
6. Have you lost any members over a controversy of substance —such as the Vietnam war, race, dollar-for-dollar giving, etc.?
7. Have you refused to build a building in the last 5 years?
8. Have you been in the press in the last year for anything other than religious advertising, potlucks, or pottery classes?
9. Have you refused to split your congregation in 2, one for "the early service" (modern), and one for "the regular service" (traditional)?
10. Have you let women and youth usher?
11. As a small symbol of voluntary servanthood, does your

church pay taxes? Not "a contribution in lieu of taxes" but the full shot?

If you answer Yes to half or more of the above, call me collect. You have one of the hottest churches in America.

TWO

How to Plan

I

There are three elements to any plan. *FIRST* is the *strategic or overall plan.* The minister decides *what* he wants the church to do. ("He" not "she" because there are notoriously few women clergy.) Note that it is the *minister* who decides. That is the way Alfred Sloan ran General Motors and it is the way the minister runs the church. Somebody has to be charged with charting the course of the ship. That is the job of the President of the United States. He cannot pass the buck to anyone. "The buck stops here" read a sign on Truman's desk.

This does not mean the minister cannot get help from any and all. Obviously he does. He would be an idiot if he didn't. But some*one* has to say, "Look, this is what I, your chief executive officer, want us to do in the next 1,3,5 years. Where am I right? Where am I wrong? How could we say it better?"

There are some tricks to strategic planning. *One,* a plan has to be written. The shorter the better. A sentence may be too long for the goal. A phrase may be better—so it will be remembered. Says linebacker Jim Marshall of the Minnesota Vikings: "Our job is to meet at the quarterback." Then everyone will know what the goal of the congregation is. If they don't like the goal, then they can either suggest a better one or leave the church.

Two, the goal is thoroughly justified and exegeted from the Bible. This means several sermons. It also means regular mention of the goal in other sermons during the year.

Three, the goal need not be organic. It need not spring from the lifestyle of the congregation so long as it does spring from the lifestyle of the Bible. It is all a matter of how tough the minister is. 95% of the churches in America, for instance, have no idea what it means to be suffering servants, which, as we shall see, was *the* goal for Jesus. Consequently if the minister sets that as *the* goal of the congregation, he's asking for trouble. If he's tough he can handle it because it's central to the faith. If he's not tough, he may end up selling insurance.

Four, the goal must be impossible. If it is within reach it's no good. "A man's reach should exceed his grasp," Browning wrote, "or what's a heaven for?" This is one place where church and business differ. Business says, "We will increase our profits 20% this year." The church says, "We will make disciples of all nations" (Matt. 28:19). Clearly the one is possible, the other not.

Jesus was always giving impossible goals. "Walk the second mile." "Turn the other cheek." "Love your enemies." That was the *point. You* couldn't do it. If it were done at all it had to be God. "With men it *is* impossible, but not with God; for all things are possible with God" (Mark 10:27). God *is* what helps us become churches.

Five, since the goal of the congregation determines everything it does, the minister had better take plenty of time setting it. He may not have it his first day on the job. But he'd better have it his second day. This is not the place to haggle. The minister knows from his study of the Bible what the job of the church is. The President is elected *because* he has a plan. Getting there is something else. There are different routes for different churches. It is the routes that are up for grabs, not the goal. The routes are what vary with the congregation, not the goal. The routes differ with the congregation's lifestyle. Some like superhighways, some like back roads. But the goal, of becoming suffering servants, is critical for all churches. There is no compromise. There is no watering down. No time need be taken. If the minister wants time, don't hire him. If he's on the job and wants time, fire him.

Six, this means that the pulpit committee had better be absolutely clear that this is this minister's goal *before* they hire him. If they don't buy it, then they can go look for another minister. The trouble, of course, is that, over coffee in a $35,000 home, most ministers water down what they know is the right goal. And most committees never even ask the candidate what his/her goal *is.* They expect the minister to be "on the job" for 1, 3, 5, 20 years before he announces the goal. They expect the goal to be "organic," to grow naturally from the lifestyle of the congregation. That may be fine for gardening, but it's no good for the church. Jesus announced the goal of suffering love from the start. "If anyone would come after me, let him deny himself and take up his cross and follow me" (Matt. 16:24). He was in trouble for 3 years. Then it was over. That is the Christian style.

Seven, if, then, a minister is on the job and has not announced the goal, he should announce it or quit. There are no alternatives. It is either/or. The reason the church is in the mess it is in America—with 2/3 of its members either peripheral or out and only 20% of its money being given away—is that the Good News of suffering love has not been preached *by* churches because it has not been preached *to* churches. It's a tough sermon to preach. "They rose up and put him out of the city" (Luke 4:29). It was precisely the thing the scribes and Pharisees—the religious establishment—could not take. But it "turned the world upside down" (Acts 17:6). Preach it or get out.

II

SECOND is the *tactical or management plan.* The minister decides *how* he wants the church to do what it has to do to be a church. Again he is not alone in his decision-making. He has his Bible. He has his God. He has his Lord. He has his prior church. He has his seminary. He has his present church. He has the Spirit. He takes advice anywhere he can get it on how this particular congregation will work for the universal church objective, namely, becoming suffering servants.

Again, there are some tricks to tactical planning.

One, anything goes. The sky's the limit. Anything that will enable people to become suffering servants.

Two, this means a complete opening up of the planning process in local churches. Committees are fine but lots of people are finer. There is no telling where an idea will originate. Furthermore, people are more willing to do what they share in the planning of.

Three, it also means a premium on creativity. The minister's job is to free people to be creative. Anything goes—wide-open services, small groups, newsprint on every wall in the sanctuary, etc.

Four, there is a tactical plan, coming straight out of the first-century church, which has much to commend it. It is simple. It is memorable. It cuts to the heart of suffering service.

> The first church *studied.* "They devoted themselves to the apostles' teaching . . ." (Acts 2:42). A disciple is a "learner" in the root sense of the word. A discipline is a way of learning. It is impossible to respond to Christ's challenge without learning exactly what he said and exactly what he meant. This requires good hard solid work with the mind. The Christian church begins and ends with the Bible, but the Bible cannot be understood unless the Bible is studied.
>
> Second, the church *shared.* "They devoted themselves to the apostles' teaching and fellowship" (Acts 2:42). The church is perhaps the one social institution where deep sharing can take place. Where else can people be so honest? Where else can they relate to each other in such depth? "If one member suffers, all suffer together. If one member is honored, all rejoice together" (I Cor. 12:26). That is the church.
>
> Third, the church *served.* "Even as the Son of man came not to be served but to serve" (Matt. 20:28). Every church member is a minister. The word "minister" means "one who serves." In New Testament times the word for "laity" and the word for "clergy" referred to the same people. Every Christian has a

major ministry, on his job and in his home, and a minor ministry, through his church. We do not all serve the Lord in the same way, but we all serve.

Five, the minister is well advised to make the church's tactical plan equally simple and memorable. This means its main points should be kept to three. No more. The human brain in its time off from making money for Standard Oil or running a home or going to school can't remember anything more. It also means that the tactical plan, as the strategic, should be preached and repreached. It must be Biblical. If it isn't Biblical, throw it out. If it isn't memorable throw it out. Hone until it is both.

Six, revise your plan constantly. What worked one year or even one month may not work another. Anything goes to get the church to study. Anything goes to get the church to share. Anything goes to get the church to serve. But you have to plan for "anything" to happen. This means 1, 2, 3 above. It also means keeping the tactical plan up for grabs *all the time.*

Seven, training therefore is the key. First, the minister gets 2 courses in planning and creativity, and retreads them every 3 years. Either during the summer for a week or more or during the winter once a week. Through a seminary or university. Second, the minister stimulates—and irritates—the members of his church to exercise their creativity constantly. What would turn you on that we haven't done yet? What are your three hottest ideas for running this church? Why don't we eliminate the Sunday school? Why is it necessary for the women to do their thing by themselves? One of our big breakthroughs was 3 years ago when the women's association finally folded.

III

THIRD is the *operational plan.* The minister decides when things will be done and who will do them. He writes down names and dates. Obviously he doesn't do this in a vacuum. He negotiates times and people. But now he has, in writing, *what* he wants to do, *how* he wants to do it, *when* it will be done, and *who* will do it.

It is at this point that planning most often goes haywire. It is the easiest step in planning and people naturally jump to it. We ask somebody to do something *before* we have determined what he/she is to do and how he/she is to do it. It may be that the job doesn't even need to be done because it is strategically wrong. Many churches, for instance, ask men (it's always a man) to be the "building fund chairman" when it has *never* (sic) been determined that the building is strategically right. It may very well be strategically wrong. How do you justify more buildings for affluent American church people when half the world goes to bed hungry? Is that the church as suffering servant? The only way to justify a new church building in the 1970s is to give at least as much to people who need it more. Thus if a church wants to build a $250,000 "new sanctuary," the "building fund drive" will be for $500,00, with the other $250,000 going where it is needed *more.*

Has the church decided that? Has it even raised the question? Strategic planning *must* come before operational. Jesus "set his face to go to Jerusalem" (Luke 9:51). But that was after he had decided his role was the suffering servant. He also decided, once he got to Jerusalem, that, operationally, far from *building* the temple it had to be cleansed and its destruction predicted. American churches must justify new buildings to the Suffering Servant. And if they can't, they'd better not build.

Again, there are some tricks to operational planning.

One, find the right person for the job. People are generally willing, and if the minister asks them to do something they usually will. Therefore the minister *(a)*must know the potential of each member and *(b)*must not fill a job until the person has agreed to the job description.

Two, write the job description. It *must* be in writing. It must not be more than one page (otherwise you will never get a volunteer to do anything). And it must be written by the chief executive officer, namely, the minister. If he can't write job descriptions, don't hire him as your minister. If he is your minister and is not writing job descriptions have him write them or quit. It is his job to know *what* he wants done; *how* he wants it done; *when* he wants it done; and *whom* he wants to do it. That is why you hired him. You hired him to *move* your church.

Now again, this is not to say the minister doesn't get help. Obviously he does. He would be an egomaniac if he didn't. But he is the one responsible, after consulting with as many people as necessary, for writing that one-page job description:

1. *What* we want you to do.
2. *How* we want you to do it.
3. *Who* we want you to get to help.
4. *When* we want you to finish.

Again, this is not to say that the job description is not negotiated. You don't call in the vice president of a major corporation, tell him you have a job for him through his church, and here's how he is to do it. He would be insulted. The point is, you do have something on paper. He will be impressed. And you do have all the essential points covered from your point of view. This is not to say there are not more essential points. It is only to say that you, as the general manager who is hired to see the whole picture, do have your essential points covered.

Three, send the person the rewritten job description. It will incorporate his/her major points. It will incorporate any other major points you and he/she may have come up with in the course of your conversation. But you will, of course, keep the foregoing outline. You will send a carbon to the appropriate committee chairperson. And you will keep a carbon for yourself.

Four, set up monthly meetings with the person in your office. He/she is reporting to you. You are the general manager. You are the minister. This regular reporting is the only way to hold volunteers accountable. And accountability is the Achilles' heel of any volunteer effort. Their mother got sick. They went for a swim. Joe came over for a drink. Unless you hold the feet to the fire, the job just won't get done.

This is why it's a lot tougher to run a volunteer outfit than a corporation. In a corporation if a guy doesn't perform he's fired. He can and should be in church, too. But it's tougher. No one expects it. There are political problems. Not so in a corporation where it is assumed that you either perform or get axed.

The trouble with churches, of course, is that they are not run like corporations. By the same token, the trouble with corporations is that they are not run like churches. Churches could use more planning and corporations could use more feeling.

Five, an even bigger problem in churches is that ministers are not held accountable. Only rarely is there a personnel or administrative or executive committee to which he/she must answer. Only rarely is there a similar committee over him in the denomination. So the minister gets away with murder. He is allowed to run his own show. And if no one puts the heat on him to run a good show, the whole church is in trouble.

Of course the most tragic thing is that most churches *are* in trouble and don't know it. No one in the congregation—remember, the church is a volunteer, spare-time group—is smart enough or tough enough to know, let alone say, that their church could be more of a suffering servant than it is. Nobody has the guts to go to the minister and tell him he is running a darn poor show. By the same token, human nature being what it is, few have the courage to tell him he is running a good show when he is.

Six, this means that it's up to the minister to identify 1–3 people in the congregation—old, young, in-between, male, female—who will let him have it, right between the eyes. Because, mind you, they love him and they love the church. The best way to keep an operational plan operating is to keep the guy/gal who is supposed to be operating it operating. That means someone who loves you enough to criticize you. A minister should take soundings with such people 2–3 times a year.

The other way is to set up a committee for an annual "performance review." It is not a good way. Who appoints the committee? Are they involved or peripheral? What is the trust level between them and the minister? How does he know, assuming the trust level is below what it would be with his closest friends who love him enough to criticize him, how does he know one or more on the committee are not out to get him? How is that atmosphere—or even the unwitting hint of it—conducive to a frank exchange that will move the church ahead? Better to do it the 1–3 way. A guy sits down, separately, with 1–3 straight-shooters, 2–3 times a year.

THREE

How to Write a Plan for Your Church

There are any number of plans that can be devised by the Spirit for the local church. As I have said, I make no brief for this one's being the best or the only. However, it does have at least the following going for it:

One, it is simple. Anyone can understand it. There are no arcane theological words—like "arcane."

Two, it is brief. You won't go to sleep reading it .You don't need a report from the Brookings Institution to get a church to move.

Three, it is memorable. You can't forget "Study-Share-Serve." They all begin with the same letter. And they are all verbs.

Four, it is scriptural. This is the first church's *kerygma* and *didache* (Acts 2:42 *et pas.*). It is the first church's *koinonia* and *agape* (Acts 2:42 *et pas.*). And it is the first church's *diakonia* and *agape* (John 12:26 *et pas.*).

Five, it is comprehensive. Virtually everything the first church did can be comprehended under one of these three heads. This means that virtually anything a church of the 1970s wants to do to be a suffering servant can also be comprehended.

Six, it sets the goal. It is written in cement. It is there for everyone to see. This church is going to do everything to be a suffering servant.

If you don't like that goal, then don't join this church. If you're already in and don't like it, then either like it or leave.

Seven, it spells out the means of reaching the goal. These are the things we do in this church. They are the things you are *expected* to do or you don't join. Or if you're already in, you do them or "find another church." This is our style. If it's not for you, fine. Find a church whose style can turn you on for Jesus more.

Eight, it names names. The following people are responsible. If they don't like the responsiblity, then they need not take the job. If they're in the job and not taking the responsibility, then they can either take it or resign.

Nine, it fixes dates. By the end of the year so much progress will be noted. You can divide the progress into twelfths or quarters or thirds. The point is you will measure. For the first time in its history the local church will measure its progress toward agreed-on goals.

A CHURCH PLAN

Principles Observed
1. Simple enough for mother-in-law.
2. Strategic plan kept to one umbrella item only, for simplicity and focus.
3. Increasingly detailed as move from strategy through tactics to operations.
4. Must be written by the church's chief executive officer, namely, the minister or priest.

St. Luke Church Plan

I. *What* we want to do : Be a suffering servant.
II. *How* we will do it: We will study, share, serve.
III. *When* it will be done and *who* will do it: Now, everyone.

Strategic or Overall Plan

I. *What* we want to do: Be a suffering servant.
   A. Our job is to be what Jesus was, individually and collectively.
   B. It is to show the young, the poor, the black, the dispossessed, that their burden is ours.
   C. It is to challenge the old, the rich, the white, the propertied to take up their cross.
   D. It is in so doing to experience the love, joy, and peace of Christ.

Tactical or Management Plan

II. *How* we will do it: We will study, share, serve.
   Every member will study, share, serve Christ.
   Every member will think, feel, act Christ.
   Every member will use brain, heart, muscle for Christ.

   We will form a think tank for Christ.
   We will form a family for Christ.
   We will form a cadre for Christ.

   We will use our intellectual equipment.
   We will use our emotional equipment.
   We will use our behavioral equipment.
   A. We will *study* Christ.
      1. We will read the Bible.
      2. We will look for Christ.
         a. We will find him in our homes.
         b. We will find him in our community.
   B. We will *share* Christ.
      1. Personally.
         a. We will divide ourselves into small groups.
         b. We will make our large groups intimate.

       c. We will make our smallest groups, our families, intimate.

       d. We will draw others into our groups.

   2. Impersonally.

       a. We will tithe.

       b. We will give away 51% of our income.

C. We will *serve* Christ.

   1. Through social service.

       a. We will divide ourselves into task forces.

       b. We will treat symptoms.

       c. We will use 40% of our benevolences.

   2. Through social action.

       a. We will divide ourselves into cadres.

       b. We will treat causes.

       c. We will use 60% of our benevolences.

       d. We will organize for social change.

          1. Through companies.

          2. Through political parties.

          3. Through the church.

          4. Through other institutions.

Operational Plan

  III. *When* it will be done and *who* will do it: Now, everyone.

    A. When: 1973

      1. *Study*

        a. By the end of 1973, 100% of the church school will be given the option of the Character Research Curriculum.[1]

        b. By the end of 1973, 33% of the church school teachers will be men, 33% youth, 33% women.

        c. By the end of 1973, 80% of the senior highs will be in the youth group.

        d. By the end of 1973, 50% of the congregation will be studying the Bible.

2. *Share*
   a. Personal
      1. By the end of 1973, 60% of the congregation will be in small groups.
      2. By the end of 1973, 40% of the families will have learned how to share.
      3. By the end of 1973, at least 12 "Advances"[2] will have been held.
      4. By the end of 1973, 100% of the college-age members will have had some meaningful contact with the church.
      5. By the end of 1973, 100% of the worship services will be intimate.
      6. By the end of 1973, the participating membership will have increased by 5%, the nonparticipating by 0%.
      7. By the end of 1973, 100% of the congregation will participate in studying, sharing, serving.
   b. Impersonal
      1. By the end of 1973, 25% of all pledging units will tithe.
      2. By the end of 1973, total pledged income will have increased 20%.
      3. During 1973, all who join the church during the year will be asked to pledge to the Annual Fund and the Benevolence Fund.
      4. By the end of 1973, arrearages in the Annual Fund and the Benevolence Fund will not exceed 5%.
         i. Any who are more than 2 months behind in their Annual giving will be counseled with by a member of the Stewardship Committee.

ii. Any who are more than two months
behind in their Benevolence Fund giving will be counseled with by a member of the Benevolence Committee.

5. By the end of October, 1973, a meaningful
stewardship program will have been devised for the following:

i. Children

ii. Junior highs

iii. Senior highs

iv. College-age

The possibility of class agents will be ex-
plored.

6. By the end of May, 1973, all givers below
the average, except in cases of known need,
will be counseled with by a member of the
Stewardship Committee.

7. By the end of 1973, 51% of income will be
spent on benevolences.

8. During 1973, no money will be given away
until it is shown, in writing, how it will
multiply by attracting other money.

9. During 1973, all benevolence money will
be split 40-60 between social service and
social action.

10. During 1973, no money will be given unless the project is experiencing difficulty
obtaining funds elsewhere.

11. By the end of February, 1973, all who have
not pledged to the Benevolence Fund will
have been asked to do so.

3. *Serve*

a. Social Service

1. By the end of 1973, 25% of the congregation will be in task forces.

       2. By the end of 1973, no new task forces will have been launched.
       3. By the end of 1973, 40% of benevolences will have been spent on social service.
    b. Social Action
       1. By the end of 1973, 15% of the congregation will be in cadres (social action groups).
       2. By the end of 1973, at least one major social ill will have been attacked.
       3. By the end of 1973, 60% of benevolences will have been spent on social action.
       4. By the end of 1973, the 15% of the congregation in cadres will be divided as follows:
          i. 3% companies
         ii. 3% political parties
        iii. 3% church
        iv. 6% other institutions

B. Who: Everyone, with responsibility for seeing that it is done vested in the following:

1. *Study* (letter corresponds with letter at III.A. 1.a., page 22).
    a. Children's Education Committee
    b. Children's Education Committee
    c. Youth-Adult Education Committee
    d. Youth-Adult Education Committee

2. *Share* (letters and numbers correspond).
    a. Personal
       1. Youth-Adult Committee
       2. Youth-Adult Committee
       3. Youth-Adult Committee
       4. Youth-Adult Committee
       5. Worship Committee
       6. New-Member Committee
       7. Membership Committee

    b. Impersonal
        1. Stewardship Committee
        2. Stewardship Committee
        3. Stewardship Committee
        4. Stewardship Committee
        5. Stewardship Committee
        6. Stewardship Committee
        7. Benevolence Committee
        8. Benevolence Committee
        9. Benevolence Committee
        10. Benevolence Committee
        11. Benevolence Committee
3. *Serve* (letters correspond).
    a. Social Service Committee
    b. Social Action Committee

FOUR

The Church as Suffering Servant

Why should the goal of suffering service be *the* goal for the church in the 1970s? Why should the image of Christ as the suffering servant be *the* image for the church in the 1970s?

I

Because it was *the* image for the church in the first 70s.

> He . . . emptied himself [Paul wrote] taking the form of a servant.
> . . . He humbled himself and became obedient unto death, even death
> on a cross (Phil. 2:7–8).

The Messiah became the Servant. The image of the king was powerful but not powerful enough. There was a greater power than the power of power. It was the power of the suffering servant. The servant was mightier than the king.

It was the oldest Christology.[1] That one man should die for many. That his suffering would heal them. That "the great shepherd of the sheep" (Heb. 13:20) would give his life to save the sheep.

> The most significant fact about the role of Jesus [writes a scholar] is
> that his mission was thought of in terms derived from the image of the
> Servant of the Lord; that he had come to seek and to save the lost; to

heal the spiritually sick; and to do wonders among men as one in whom
and through whom the Spirit of God was at work (Mark 1:10, 23f.;
2:17; 10:45; Luke 7:22; 19:10).[2]

Peter speaks of Jesus as the servant (Acts 3:13). The first preachers
speak of Jesus as the servant (Acts 4:30). Paul calls Jesus servant
(Phil. 2:7). Mark, the earliest Gospel, speaks of Jesus as coming not
to be served but to serve (Mark 10:45). It stays through the later
Matthew: "Behold my servant whom I have chosen" (Matt. 12:15).
Through the later Luke in Jesus' first sermon (Luke 4:18f.). Through
the later John: "Jesus should die for the nation" (John 11:51).
Through Hebrews and Jesus' gift of himself (Heb. 9:26). Through
Revelation and the sacrifice of the Lamb (Rev. 5:12 *et pas.*).

They could only have gotten it from Jesus himself.

> He has sent me to proclaim release to the captives
> and recovering of sight to the blind,
> to set at liberty those who are oppressed,
> to proclaim the acceptable year of the Lord (Luke 4:18–19).

> The Son of man . . . came . . . to give his life
> as a ransom for many (Mark 10:45).

> This cup is the new covenant in my
> blood (1 Cor. 11:25).

The point of his temptations was that he refused to be a nonsuffering
servant. The point of his life was that he would give it up. The point
of his death was that the suffering would release the power as the king
could never do.

He could only have gotten it from deep within his tradition. It went
all the way back to Moses, who was prepared to give his life for his
people (Exod. 32:32). It went back to 600 B.C. when an unknown poet
wrote one of the most startling things in the history of the world:

> He was despised and rejected by men;
> a man of sorrows, and acquainted with grief;
> and as one from whom men hide their faces
> he was despised, and we esteemed him not (Isa. 53:3).

The strand of suffering lay deep within the tradition. Jesus repristinated it. He merged the two traditions of Servant and Messiah. It had never been done before. It was his genius. It was his power.

> Jesus [writes an expert] conceived of his mission as that of the servant of the Lord whom Isaiah had foretold.[3]

> The primitive church's conception of the messiahship of Jesus [writes another] owes much to [Isa. 42:1, 61:1], no doubt because he had himself interpreted his mission in terms of the Servant. . . .[4]

II

So had the first church their mission. They too were servants of the Lord. They too would suffer. They too would die. Suffering service was *the* goal for the church in the first 70s.

> If any man would come after me, let him deny himself and take up his cross and follow me (Matt. 16:24).

That was the way you were a Christian. That was your job as a Christian. That was what you did if you were a Christian.

> I will show him how much he must suffer for the sake of my name (Acts 9:16).

And Paul suffered.

> The same experience of suffering is required of your brotherhood throughout the world (1 Pet. 5:9).

To deny yourself *is* to suffer. To take up your cross *is* to suffer. A cross *is* a symbol of suffering. That is why it has lasted.

> The kingdom of the Lamb [writes an expert] is established through suffering, and the reign of the saints as manifest on earth is expressed through self-sacrifice and service.[5]

They even called themselves servants.

> Paul, a servant of Jesus Christ (Rom. 1:1).
> James, a servant of God and . . . Christ (James 1:1).

> Peter, a servant . . . of Jesus Christ (2 Pet. 1:1).
> Jude, a servant of . . . Jesus Christ (Jude 1:1).
> Grant to thy servants [they prayed] to speak thy word with all boldness
> (Acts 4:29).

Why? Why this emphasis on servanthood? Because servanthood
was power. It reduced a person to the point where he could be used,
and at that point he became effective for Christ. At that point Christ
became effective. It was the key to his effectiveness.

> He humbled himself and became obedient unto death. . . . Therefore
> God has highly exalted him (Phil. 2:8–9).

The key to Christ's power was his weakness. Weakness is more powerful than power. The suffering servant is more powerful than the
messiah. The church member as suffering servant is more powerful
than the church member as layperson or minister.

Now plenty of people encounter suffering. The Servant used suffering to accomplish his work. He used it not to save himself but to save
others. That is how powerful love to the uttermost is.

> Surely he has borne *our* griefs
>   and carried *our* sorrows; . . .
> Upon him was the chastisement that made *us* whole,
>   and with his stripes *we* are healed (Isa. 53:4–5).

That moves *us* to repent. It moves *us* to suffer. It moves *us* to serve.
That is how powerful suffering service is. The first Christians were
dumfounded—first by what Christ had done and then by what *they*
were doing.

> Are they servants of Christ? I am a better one—I am talking like a
> madman—with far greater labors, far more imprisonments, with
> countless beatings, and often near death. Five times I have received at
> the hands of the Jews the forty lashes less one. Three times I have been
> beaten with rods; once I was stoned. Three times I have been ship-
> wrecked; a night and a day I have been adrift at sea . . . (2 Cor.
> 11:23–25).

It was effective. He used the example of his own suffering service to win people for Christ. They all did. It was that powerful. They knew they had what the world had been longing for. They knew *it* had *them*. And in that grip was power. "These men," exclaimed a mob as they dragged them before the authorities, "have turned the world upside down" (Acts 17:6).

III

All right. But just because it's in the Bible doesn't mean it's right.

Of course. There's a lot in the Bible that's wrong. There are errors in fact. Errors in text. Errors in who said what to whom and when. But there is no error on the big things. And this is the biggest. That God so loved the world (John 3:16) that he gave first a nation and then a man as examples of his suffering love. And that that suffering love is the hope of the world. *That* theme has stuck.

Not only because it's in the Bible. But because it's in us. The brilliance of the Bible is that it recreates all the big themes that have used us for centuries. And this is the biggest. That there is something in us calling us to give ourselves in love to the uttermost. That that something *is* God. That God will win. And that his victory is proved by the Exodus. Proved by the Resurrection. And proved by us whenever we love to the point where we too suffer. Or proved by someone else whenever he or she loves us to the point where he or she suffers for us.

The goal of suffering service is *the* goal for the church in the 1970s not only because it was for the first church in the first 70s but because it is a goal that works in the 1970s. It has worked for *you*. When someone other person laid himself or herself aside for you, that was when it happened. You knew you were in touch with the ultimate in power. By *their* stripes *you* were healed.

*

Second objection. We act only out of self-interest. Do we? It was not in Moses' self-interest to lead the people out of Israel. But he did it. Even though it meant the suffering of rejection, doing what he didn't want to do, failing.

It was not in Elijah's self-interest to go back to his people. But he went. Even though there was a price on his head.

It was not in Paul's self-interest to go back to his friends and tell them he had turned Christian. That's like going back to your friends and telling them you've turned communist. But he went.

Ah, but these are all geniuses. Were they? Moses, doubtful of his own ability. Elijah, a nobody from nowhere. Paul, at war with himself (Rom. 7:23). Jesus, in a rage of doubt (Luke 22:44).

Ah, but they were only individuals. Were they? Moses organized a nation. Elijah helped keep it together. Paul carried the good news about the Servant all over the world. The Servant himself accounts for a third of the world embracing servanthood. First, they did what was most certainly not in their self-interest. Second, they got people to join up on tough, servanthood terms.

Ah, but we don't have leaders like that any more. Not so. They're all over. More specifically: they're in us. *We* know that the message of Christianity is the cross. *We* know that the message of the cross is self-sacrifice. *We* know that we are expected to be suffering servants.

*

Third objection. All right. So you get one or two people. But you can't get the whole *church* to be suffering servants.

Why not? Jesus did. They were his *terms.* They still are. He said, "Follow me." He didn't say, You'll make more money. He didn't say, You'll meet a lot of nice people. He didn't promise them anything. He did the opposite of promise. He said, "If any man would come after me, let him *deny* himself and take up his *cross* and follow me."

The trouble with the church in the 1970s is precisely that it promises too much and challenges too little. The political party promises its platform. The school promises an education. The bank promises interest. The therapy group promises fulfillment.

What does the church promise? *Nothing.* It is the only organization you join because you are promised nothing but challenged everything. Go the second mile. Turn the other cheek. Love your enemies. pray for those who persecute you. What kind of promises are those? They are promises of suffering. Join us and you are in for a tough, hard ride.

*

Fourth objection. The goal, then, is self-maximization, not suffering service. You do the tough things to become the person you were meant to be.

Perhaps. Good objection. But perhaps not. You don't *know* it's going to turn out that way. The self-maximization may occur, but then again it may not. Jesus didn't go to the cross to maximize himself. He went because he was ordered. He was a servant. He would obey. "He learned obedience through what he suffered," an early Christian explained (Heb. 5:8). The point was the obedience, not the self-fulfillment. The self-fulfillment, if it came at all, was a by-product. We have it backward. You don't join a church for self-fulfillment from which you may or may not be moved to suffering service. You join a church for suffering service from which you may or may not get self-fulfillment.

The church offers a radically *different* kind of organization. It is precisely when the church tries to duplicate the Rotary Club and the precinct caucus that it gets into trouble. You join the church because you want something different. Radically different. You want something that isn't your lifestyle. That goes against your grain. That isn't in your self-interest. And it isn't *you* who wants it. It *has* to be God because it *couldn't* be you. That is not all God is. But God is at least that. God is what gets you to join an organization that offers you nothing in your own self-interest. At least not now. Not immediately. Not right away. Not that you can see.

The trouble with the church is that it *isn't* different. We have people sliding into churches all the time and never noticing any difference. It's the same thing you can get anywhere else—and get better. The school's a better school. The bank's a better bank. (It certainly pays more.) The club's a better club. The therapy group's a better therapy group.

The problem is that the church has chosen all the wrong models. It has modeled itself on the Chamber of Commerce but it has not modeled itself on the Suffering Servant. We use organizational models that we are comfortable with. We even elect people to run our churches who are most comfortable with those organizational models. We use models, in other words, that we know from our experience will work.

But work for what? For self-interest. We are afraid to risk the only model that will work for everybody's interest. And that is the model of the suffering servant. And on that model no one has a corner. Perhaps least of all the people who are geared up to run highly efficient self-interest models 40 to 80 hours a week. We need more mothers running our churches and fewer executives. We need more blacks and fewer whites. We need more youth and fewer ministers.

*

Fifth objection. Nobody ever suffers enough.

Quite right. We must watch the danger of pharisaism—namely, that I'm better than you because I suffer more than you, which, of course, I don't. There are varying degrees of suffering in the church. But that is not the point. The point is not that we do not suffer enough but that *we do not suffer at all.*

If it is true that Christians are those who do what Christ did and give themselves in love to the uttermost, then it follows that a church is not a church until it does that. Since very few churches in America do it, there are very few *churches* in America.

Moses obeyed orders at great risk to himself. So did Elijah. So did Jesus. So did Paul. Joining the church is a risky business. Can you imagine new-member committees telling potential members: You are joining this church for one reason only, to give yourself in love to the uttermost? If that causes you inconvenience, fine. If it isn't inconvenient, then it isn't *that* kind of love. In simple language, we are asking you to sacrifice. If you want to join us but don't want to sacrifice, then don't join. We want your time. We want your money. We want yourself. Then together we will do something we never dreamed would be possible. We will give the world an example of suffering service because such examples are the world's hope.

Make no mistake: this is what the church is coming to. It is the only way the church is going to make it out of the century. The church as a social appendix will be replaced by the church as a suffering servant.

Make no mistake: this is not for everyone. Jesus began with 12. It went down to 11. At the end three Gospel writers say there were none, one says there was one. This is not for everyone. People do not join organizations to deny themselves. They do not join organizations to take up their cross. They do not join to suffer. Churches are losing members all over the country. It couldn't be a better sign.

*

Sixth objection. The emphasis on suffering service is masochistic.

Not so. You don't go into it for the suffering. You go in for the service. You don't go in because you want to get hurt. You go in because you want to obey. "Take up your cross." Why do you want to obey? Because you see the man on the cross as the only thing, in your experience, powerful enough to blast *you* out of *your* self-interest. Yes, someone else may have done it for you. But it is entirely possible, if not probable, that that person in turn was motivated by the man on the cross. That man and that way you see as the hope of the world.

Now there are obviously plenty of other hopes. The democracies have theirs. The communists have theirs. The Moslems theirs. The Buddhists theirs. We must not denigrate others' hopes. On the other hand, what we must do is push ours. If Christ is, as we say, "the hope of the world"; if that is to say, the suffering love he displayed is the hope of *the* world because it has worked in *our* world; then we must push that kind of love. More accurately: we must show it.

This is where the creativity of churches is most missed and least encouraged. What has *your* church done to show the world *that* kind of love? Precious little. A new red rug to the altar. A stained-glass window. A pittance to missions. Silence or lateness on the great social issues. Mortgages for buildings but no mortgages for benevolences. From now on *anything* goes in *any* church to show suffering service.

Far from being masochistic, it brings joy.

> Rejoice [Peter said] in so far as you share Christ's sufferings (1 Pet. 4:13).

> Rejoice [Jesus said] and be glad [when you are persecuted] (Matt. 5:12).

> We rejoice in our sufferings [Paul wrote] (Rom. 5:3).

> Count it all joy, my brethren, [James said] when you meet various trials (Jas. 1:2).

Why? Because they were sharing in the suffering of Christ, which was, which is, the hope of the world.

*

Seventh objection. Granted that we may go along with all this intellectually, it is hard to go along with it emotionally. In other words, while we applaud it, we won't *do* it.

Precisely. That is the point. *We* won't do it. I can write it, but I can't live it. Whenever even approximations occur, they *have* to be God, they can't be me. Why? Because I know myself and I know that I am primarily motivated by self-interest. It is the human condition. It is sin.

The point of suffering service is that *we* cannot be suffering servants. The church are the people organized around an impossibility. We can't do it. Not on our own. It is done through us, not by us. That's where the church gets its power. We *are* organized. We *are* saved. We *are* loved. It is the power of the passive. Since no one ever serves enough, we have to *be* saved. We cannot save ourselves. And the point of signing up for suffering service is to prove to ourselves that we cannot save ourselves. That we have to *be* saved. And that in God's suffering love we *are* saved.

God shows his love for us in that while we were yet sinners Christ died for us (Rom. 5:8).

My church [a member wrote] has stretched me so much. I find myself doing things that were beyond me before.

Beyond me, yes, that's the point. They *are* beyond you. They *have* to be God. Because they *can't* be you.

And they are all that matter, aren't they, these acts of suffering love? You can have all the money, all the power, all the fame, all the self-interest things in the world. But if you have not loved until you too have suffered, what are you? And then you die. And what is left? We only have what we give. That's Christianity. That's the church.

FIVE

The Church Studies

"They devoted themselves to the apostles' teaching" (Acts 2:42). It was one of the ways they spelled out their goal of suffering service. The only way you could know about suffering service was to learn about the Suffering Servant. That meant being taught. It meant the scriptures.

I

Most of us resist the Bible. Our objections go something like this. *First* objection. I cannot understand it. But that's ridiculous. Of course you can understand it. All you have to do is the following.

One, get an edition you can read. That means one on which you don't have to use a magnifying glass.

Two, get an edition in a modern language. There is no sense being saddled with a Bible translated in 1611 unless the old language makes more sense to you. Get the Revised Standard Version. It is everyone's basic Bible. It is up to date. It is accurate. It is readable. Then get as many other versions of the Bible as you find helpful. *The Cottonpatch Version of Luke and Acts. Letters to Street Christians. Good News for Modern Man.* They are available in any church library. Better yet, they're in any church bookrack. Be sure they're in yours.

Three, get a commentary. Get a readable expert who breaks it all down for you: who said what, to whom, why, when, under what circumstances. The most valuable for the New Testament is William Barclay's *Daily Study Bible.* And the most valuable for the entire Bible is the Abingdon "One-Volume Commentary." Again, all available through your church.

*

Second objection. I don't have the time.

But that, of course, is not true. We always have time for what we feel is important. If we don't have time for the Bible, then we don't feel the Bible is important. It's just that simple.

Why is the Bible important? Because it was for the first Christians. We wouldn't be reading books like this now if they hadn't studied then. "They received the word with all eagerness, examining the scriptures daily to see if these things were so" (Acts 17:11). One of the marks of the teaching, or *didache* as it was called, was the constant reference to scripture.[1] "Let the word of God dwell in you richly as you teach and admonish one another in all wisdom" (Col. 3:16).

It was important for Jesus. He was brought up on it. He was taught the alphabet so he could read the Bible. All Jewish boys were.[2] The first thing we read about his ministry was that he taught from the scriptures in the synagogues.[3] Throughout the Gospels he makes constant reference to the prophets and the law.

The Bible is also important because it is our cultural heritage. The Pilgrims left England because they wanted to read their Bibles and worship the way *they* wanted to read their Bibles and worship. Our country is founded on the Judeo-Christian tradition and the Judeo-Christian tradition is found in the Bible. Many would argue that the reason we are in the trouble we are in our country is that we have not paid sufficient attention to our cultural heritage. A tree that is all branches and no roots dies.

*

Third objection. O.K. So I should read the Bible. It is important.

I agree. As a matter of fact, I couldn't agree more. I'll even send my children to Sunday school to read it. But as for actually taking the time myself, I'm human, and I won't. It's not that I don't have the time. It's that I won't take the time.

That's phony. At least when I use that kind of argument I know it's phony for me. For years I used to say to myself, "All my life I've wanted to play the guitar." And it was true. I had. But I didn't begin to play the guitar until two years ago when someone called me on my phoniness. "Look," I was told, "either you want to play the guitar or you don't. If you do, I'll help you. If you don't, quit talking about it." The next day I found myself, in fear and trembling, standing before the guitars at Schmitt Music.

The church are the people who call us on our phoniness. If we're really serious about the Bible, people in churches say to each other, then we *will* take the time for it. Otherwise let's admit that we really are *not* serious, because we *won't* take the time.

*

Fourth objection. It's not my job. I hire someone to read the Bible for me and explain it to me. He's the expert. I'm not. It's his job. Not mine.

Nonsense. We're all experts. No one has a corner on the Bible. It can speak to any of us. It does. "Teach and admonish *one another* in all wisdom."

We have to watch the specialization syndrome that afflicts so much of American life. Buckminster Fuller has suggested that overspecialization is what brings down a species. I run my company; the minister reads my Bible. I run my home; the minister runs my Bible. I do my schoolwork; the minister does my Bible. It is a false dichotomy. If the Bible had been left to the clergy the entire Christian enterprise would have folded long ago. When the Bible *was* left to the clergy, they did such choice things as burn the people who dared to translate it so others could read it.

Having said that, however, it *is* the minister's job to get people reading their Bibles. He must cajole, browbeat, wheedle, and inspire to the point where they *will* take the time. That is his job. It is what he is paid for. He is also paid to be a peripatetic commentary. He is paid to help people understand what they read. Presumably he was trained to do so. The sad fact of the matter is, however, that most ministers do not know the original languages the way a doctor, say, knows the original anatomy. If we want to get the church to study the Bible, we might well begin by getting the seminarians to study the Hebrew and the Greek.

*

Fifth objection to reading the Bible. It is irrelevant. The only thing that matters is whether I lead "a good Christian life." And I can do that without reading the Bible.

Can you? Much of what passes for the "good Christian life" is just good Christian convenience. How can you *know* what the good Christian life *is* apart from the book which tells you what it is? You may not be leading a good Christian life. Are you a suffering servant? Do you love to the uttermost? Have you given yourself? Are you used?

How can you say you're leading "a good Christian life" when you haven't gotten your church, which is presumably the avatar of good Christian living, to spend as much money on others as it spends on itself? How can you say you're leading "a good Christian life" when you haven't won one person for Christ, which is what it's all about? But you wouldn't know that if you hadn't read to the end of Matthew.

As usual, humor puts this kind of objection in perspective. When a South Sea Islander proudly showed an American soldier his Bible during World War II, the G.I. said with disdain, "We've outgrown that sort of thing, you know." "It's a good thing *we* haven't," the Islander replied. "If it wasn't for this book, you'd have been a meal by now."

*

Sixth objection. I don't know where to start.

Where do you start with the newspaper? Page 1? Sports page?

Comics? Editorials? Start anywhere. Only start at the beginning of a book. People get upset with the Bible because they open it in the middle of a book and expect it to make sense. That doesn't work for novels and it doesn't work for Bibles.

*

Seventh objection. I don't like what the Bible is telling me to do.

Now we are getting down to it. This is the real reason many of us don't read the Bible. Who wants to be a suffering servant? Who wants to take up his cross? Who wants to deny himself? Who wants to go the second mile, turn the other cheek, love the enemy, pray for the persecutor? We don't want to read the Bible, not because it's hard to read but because it's hard to *do.*

That's why we need support groups. I am not at all sure that the Bible, unlike other books, can be read alone. The church are the people who read the Bible. Together. "You teach . . . one another." We do together what we cannot do as well alone. It's not that we won't read it alone. It's that we won't *do* it alone. It is too much. It is too hard. It is too contrary to our self-interest. We will not do what the Bible is telling us to do without pressure from our friends to do it. And what it tells us to do is so radically different from anything we have ever been told to do before that we *can't* do it without their love. The church are the people who love each other into doing what the Bible tells them to do.

A church's first job is to get its people reading the Bible. Many churches have support groups, all right. But what do they support? People in pain. People in joy. And that's beautiful as far as it goes. But what about the Bible? Do they support each other trying to *do* the Bible? Trying to *be* suffering servants?

So often you hear of churches "split down the middle." But the split is invariably over a non-servanthood, non-Biblical issue. Do you remember the church in New Mexico that split over how to park on Sunday morning? Some wanted to park straight-in. Others wanted to park diagonally. You could even tell which was which by the way they sat in their pews on Sunday morning. The straight-in-ers sat straight and the diagonal-ers sat diagonally.

We need more churches split down the middle over Biblical issues. We need people so turned on by what the Bible is telling them to do that they inflame other people. That other people catch their fire. That together they become what their founder was, a suffering servant. How are you going to know that unless you read it? And how are you going to read it unless you have a church? Unless you are a church?

I never used to read the Bible any more than the next person. I wasn't even committed to being a minister. Then I found myself in a seminary on a scholarship for a year just to think about whether or not this was for me. And I came in touch with one of the most remarkable human beings I have ever known. He was a professor of Old Testament. He lived it. Breathed it. Ate it. Slept it. He was a legend in his own time. And in a chapel service on September 25, 1958, that man said something which sums it up: "Go to your Bibles and listen."

It took with me. *He* took with me. It was all because of him. I went to him. He was my group. He was my *church*. He brought me his fire. And in a sense everything I have ever done since is a result of that transference of fire. I even dedicated one of my own books to him because he had dedicated his book, the Bible, to me. And to thousands of other young people like me. Who became older people. But who never lost his fire.

A minister's job is to inflame people with the Bible. If a minister did nothing else but hook people on the Bible he would be in business as a minister because the rest would follow. "Go to your Bibles and listen." You are bound to come back a suffering servant. You are bound to come back on fire.

II

Why do you read the Bible? Not because the first church did. Not because Jesus did. Not because the Pilgrims did. What kind of reasons are those? You read the Bible because you can't *help* reading the

Bible. It is that powerful. It comes to *you*. You do not come to it. Of
course you can't understand it. Of course you won't take the time. Of
course somebody else could read it better. Of course it's irrelevant and
you don't know where to start and you don't like what it's telling you
to do. That's the *point*. It's the proof that it isn't *you* who are doing
the reading. The reading is going on in spite of you. Left to your own
devices, you wouldn't read it. That's obvious. That's demonstrated.
It's *a priori* and *a posteriori* both. It's Q.E.D. It's you. Left to our own
devices we won't read the Bible. That's the *point*. We are *not* left to
our own devices.

> The word of God is living and active, sharper than any two-edged
> sword, piercing to the division of soul and spirit, of joints and marrow,
> and discerning the thoughts and intentions of the heart (Heb. 4:12).

It isn't that the word of God in the Bible and elsewhere is important. It isn't that we should read it. It's that the word of God is *alive*
and is reading *us*.[4] That sounds mystical? Fine. That's not the way you
run your company? Good. That's not your style? Excellent. If it were
your style it wouldn't be the Bible. That's the point. Not that we read
the Bible but that the Bible reads *us*. We are passive. We are in its
grip. We are drawn to it like filings to a magnet. You aren't drawn?
Of course you're drawn. Why do you go to church? Why will you go
back next week? Why are you hungry for more? More to the point:
Why do you find yourself doing the word that you hear?

Because you can't help doing it. That is how powerful the word is.
To "hear" in the Hebrew meant to "obey." You don't read it, you hear
it. You don't hear it, you say it. And you don't say it, you do it. The
word is so powerful it has within it the seeds of its own accomplish-
ment. Mystical? You bet. But powerful.[5] It is God.[6] God *is* what you
find yourself doing, that *you* would never have done, in response to
a word *you* would never have read.

> As the rain . . . giv[es] seed to the sower and bread to the eater,
> so shall my word be that goes forth from my mouth;
>   it shall not return to me empty,

> but it shall accomplish that which I purpose,
> and prosper in the thing for
> which I sent it (Isa. 55:10–11).

God does not reveal information; he reveals his will. The words are not data; they are commands. We are in their grip. We are in their power. We are *over*powered. We are passive. We are inflamed.

> Is not my word like fire, says the Lord, and like a hammer which breaks the rock in pieces? (Jer. 23:29)

That was how powerful the word was.

> And God said, "Let there be light"; and there was (Gen. 1:3).

That was how powerful the word was.

> You have been born anew . . . through the living . . . word of God (1 Pet. 1:23).

That is how power-less we are before the onslaught of the word. It is the epitome of the passive. Nobody has anything to do with his birth.

You don't read the Bible because you could, should, or would. You read the Bible because you can't help reading the Bible. Then you do, not what you read but what you heard. Not because you could or should or would. But because you can't help doing it.

> For this commandment which I command you this day is not too hard for you, neither is it far off. . . . But the word is very near you; it is in your mouth and in your heart, *so that you can do it* (Deut. 30:14).

SIX

The Church Shares

You can think all the right thoughts. You can say all the right words. You can even do all the right things. But the church is not the church until you feel it.

"They devoted themselves to the apostles' . . . fellowship" (Acts 2:42). When Luke said that, he used a word that went back to his cultural roots. It meant to share something in common.[1] It meant to give and receive. It meant to be so close to someone you were a business partner. It meant to be so close you were a fellow citizen. It meant to be so close you were friends. It meant to be so close you were married.

I

FIRST, there was the fellowship with God. It went all the way back. "I will be with you" (Exod. 3:12). It was the heart of the "covenant." It was what distinguished the Hebrew religion. To be sure there was distance. It was the root of the word "holy."[2]

> Do not come near; put off your shoes from your feet, for the place on which you are standing is holy ground (Exod. 3:5).

Nevertheless the point of the religion was the closeness of the God.

When Israel was a child, I loved him
and out of Egypt I called my son. . . .
I . . . taught Ephraim to walk.
  I took them up in my arms. . . .
I led them with cords of compassion,
  with the bands of love,
and I became to them as one
  who eases the yoke on their jaws,
    and I bent down to them and fed them (Hos. 11:1, 3, 4).

II

SECOND, there was the fellowship with the Holy Spirit. "The fellowship of the Holy Spirit be with you all" (2 Cor. 13:14). It was what we might call the fellowship of the passive. It bound all those who were being used. It bound the believers. It bound the church. The church *were* the people whom the Spirit brought together. They were the called (1 Cor. 1:9). The chosen (John 15:16). The gripped:

> And suddenly a sound came from heaven like the rush of a mighty wind, and it filled all the house where they were sitting. . . . And they were all filled with the Holy Spirit (Acts 2:2, 4).

III

THIRD, there was the fellowship with Christ. He was dead, to be sure, but the fellowship was such that he would not die. It was unbelievable. But that was not important. What was important was that you could *feel* it. It was that close. *He* was that close.

> I have been crucified with Christ; it is no longer *I* who live, but Christ who lives in me . . . who loved *me* and gave himself for *me* (Gal. 2:20).

Implausible as it may seem, they felt closest to him in his suffering.[3] They had this idea—this idea had them, this *feeling* had them—that the Christian life was a sharing in the sufferings of Christ.

> Rejoice in so far as you share Christ's sufferings (1 Pet. 4:13).

> I rejoice in my sufferings for your sake, and in my flesh I complete what

is lacking in Christ's afflictions for the sake of his body, that is, the church (Col. 1:24).

It was for a reason. It was the only way, they felt, to keep the closeness. You aren't close until you share someone's suffering. Then you are so close that it will last.

> That I may share his sufferings, becoming like him in his death, that if possible I may attain the resurrection from the dead (Phil. 3:11).

> We are . . . fellow heirs with Christ *provided* we suffer with him *in order that* we may also be glorified with him (Rom. 8:17).

> If we have been united with him in a death like his, we shall certainly be united with him in a resurrection like his (Rom. 6:5).

In other words, the first church had a feeling, the feeling had them, that their fellowship with Christ was so close that they could suffer and take it, they could die and be raised, they could live and rejoice. They were changed. They had *been* changed. They were new (John 3:7; Rom. 6:4; Gal. 6:15).

> If any one is in Christ, he is a new creation; the old has passed away, behold, the new has come. All this is from God (2 Cor. 5:17–18).

God *was* what made them new.

> It is no longer I who live, but Christ who lives in me.

God *was* what made them *that* close.

IV

FOURTH, there was the fellowship with each other. It was a demonstration of the unbelievable *koinonia.* One evidence of the newness was that you had a new relationship to people. One evidence of the change was that you would even suffer for them. Not just with them but for them.

> Greater love has no man than this, that a man lay down his life for his friends (John 15:13).

I rejoice in my sufferings for your sake (Col. 1:24).

It was kind of you to share my trouble (Phil. 4:14).

You share in our sufferings (2 Cor. 1:7).

Recall the former days when, after you were enlightened, you endured a hard struggle with sufferings, sometimes being publicly exposed to abuse and affliction, and sometimes being partners with those so treated. For you had compassion on the prisoners . . . (Heb. 10:32–34).

If one member suffers, all suffer together; if one member is honored, all rejoice together (1 Cor. 12:26).

The church are the people who share that much. Who are that close. Who are that eager to catch feeling up to thinking. Who are that eager to catch feeling up to acting. Who want to share as well as study and serve.

Bear one another's burdens, and so fulfil the law of Christ (Gal. 6:2).

The sorrows of one are the sorrows of all. The joys of one are the joys of all. My tears are your tears and your laughter mine. It was so powerful a *feeling* that one expert says it was "the binding force that held the church together."[4]

The "beloved community"[5] are the people who can be themselves and be for each other and risk a great deal as they learn how to feel.

The people of St. Luke [reads a letter to a church] have given me something which I can never lose . . . not an education in Presbyterianism, not new knowledge of the wonderful miracles of Christ, but they have given me a chance to be me. They have given me fellowship, encouragement, love, acceptance, a feeling of importance, goals to strive for. . . .

Isn't that what it's all about?

How are ya [reads another from a teenager who moved away]? I thought you might appreciate seeing a "menu" and a bulletin from the church I visited. I am thinking of joining and attempt to put in a little of St. Luke. I'm sure it would be an improvement. Boy, I sure do miss that church with all those wonderful people in it. . . .

Or this?

I sit through church all soft inside, thrilled up and down my spine, overcome with gratitude for youth and young people, and deeply grateful for the ministry of St. Luke.

But it wasn't just the large group and worship. It wasn't just the small group and the sharing of burdens. It was a fellowship so close that they even gave their money to each other. The word for "sharing" was the same as the word for "giving."

You will glorify God by . . . the generosity of your contribution (2 Cor. 9:13).

Macedonia and Achaia have been pleased to make some contribution for the poor among the saints at Jerusalem (Rom. 15:26).

Again and again he referred to it. They had been transformed by the fellowship.

And they sold their possessions and goods and distributed them to all, as any had need (Acts 2:45).

It was unheard of.

I'm going back to work next week [said a woman in a small group meeting on the giving of money at a church]. And I pledge 10% of my income.

It was beautiful. It was feeling. It was fellowship.

I'm sure you've discussed this with the Lord [someone said]. But what about your husband?

He doesn't even know I'm going back to work.

V

FIFTH, there are, of course, objections to sharing this kind of feeling in churches. Here's how they run.

One, can't I get sharing like this with my neighbor? At my lodge? My club? At Joe's bar? With my family?

Of course. But those are very limited places. Your sharing is limited to your friends. To your age group. To your loved ones. To your class.

The Samaritan woman was out of Jesus' class. So was Zaccheus. So was Pilate. If Jesus had stuck to his own class, he would have stayed as a small businessman in Nazareth.

There are *no* limits to Christian sharing. The trouble with churches is that they are limited to one class by housing. Our own city council voted 3–3 on low-income housing. All of 30 units. I wonder what churches the three opponents belong to. Come to think of it, I wonder what political party they belong to. Or parties. Single-class churches, in other words most churches, are not particularly Christian. Why? Because they limit sharing, when Christian sharing is, by definition, *un*limited. "For God so loved the *world* . . ." (John 3:16).

No matter how backyard and single-class a local church is, it is always related to the world church, which is all-class and not limited. You can go to Joe's Bar, for instance, and not be related to the people in Fritz's Bar at a hotel in Germany. But you can't go to church and not be related to the people who go to church in Germany.

This is why a church's budget should reflect more giving to the broader church than it does. Like 25% of all benevolences.

> God was in Christ reconciling the *world* to himself. . . . So we are ambassadors for Christ, God making his appeal through us (2 Cor. 5:19–20).

Christian sharing is unlimited or it isn't Christian sharing. When you join the church you agree to extend your limits. The church are the unlimited people. Beyond the limits of class. Beyond the limits of politics. Beyond the limits of country. Beyond the limits of race.

*

Two, but isn't that artificial? You're telling me if I join the church I have to be related to black people, troubled people, low-income people.

Of course it's artificial. It was artificial for Jesus to associate with Matthew, the tax collector; with Judas, the revolutionary; with Joanna, the wife of Herod's steward (Luke 8:3). It was artificial for Paul the Jew to associate with Philemon the Greek; with Onesimus the slave; with the others in jail.

Of course it's artificial. Just the way it was artificial to leave home for kindergarten. We didn't know anybody. We were out of our depth. Out of our class. Often even out of luck. It was artificial to leave grade school for junior high, junior high for senior, senior high for college, and college for the cold, cruel world.

The point is, we're pushing to the limits of our *koinonia* all the time. Christianity says keep pushing. Do the artificial so much it becomes natural. The church is the place where you do that. The church *are* the people who do it.

What other institution in society is impelled by the same kind of urgency? Who else tells you to break down every barrier, tear down every wall? Who else says there are no walls, there are no barriers?

*

Three, O.K. But I don't see that kind of fellowship in my church.

Then either change yourself or change your church. Because if you don't have that kind of sharing then it isn't the church. "Bear one another's burdens, and so fulfil the *law* of Christ." The person who couldn't stand the word "law" made this his only law. Without the burden-bearing there was no church.

But how do you *do* that? Get in a small group. Talk with people whose lives have been changed. "My life has been changed by this church," a man said. It's a two-way street. He should say it more and we should listen more. Whenever a person says his church isn't close he is saying that he hasn't been close to his church. By the same token his church has to be so close that he can't avoid it. Can't avoid *them.* People are turned off by the church because they don't see the church doing what it is supposed to be doing—loving each other, being for each other.

A young couple came back to a church after 10 weeks away. "We're glad to be back," they said, through tears in their eyes. That's the church.

*

Four, but that's not my style. I don't divulge the deep places of my life to others. And I don't expect them to divulge theirs to me.

Why not? Have you ever tried? Remember: that kind of depth was what held the first church together. That kind of depth then is what puts us here now. That's power, and it could be argued that life is too short to miss that kind of power. It is the power of feeling.

"I like the feeling at your services," a woman said at a dinner party. This was just after another person had asked the only "Reverend" present to convert her on the spot.

*

Five, but I don't want to share someone else's suffering. I have enough of my own.

Fair enough. But why emphasize the suffering? It is there. It is essential. But it isn't all. "If one member is honored, all rejoice together." Look at the names and faces on the bulletin board of your church. Emphasize the joy. The Good News as well as the bad. That's what small and large groups, church groups, are all about.

By the same token, look hard at how much you really are suffering. You could be kidding yourself. You may not be suffering as much as you think. And you may be bearing very few other burdens. In either event, what you are bearing enables you to bear more.

> The incredible support you all give me allows me to take the risk of failing. . . . I come to church knowing that these people care about me, no matter what.

*

Six, O.K. So bearing others' burdens is fine. But it's fine only if you have, as one person put it, "nice people with interesting burdens."

What about someone who monopolizes a fellowship with a boring burden?

That's quite a commentary on where we are as Christians. It may be where we are as individuals, but if it's where we are as Christians, we have a way to go. The job of the church is to expand those limits. "All have sinned and fall short of the glory of God" (Rom. 3:23). Therefore it is presumptuous to be bored by one person's sin and exhilarated by another's.

I was going to call a church member to ask him to share something meaningful and Christian with some other people. It would have taken 24 hours of his time. I was reluctant. I called a third man and expressed my reluctance. "I don't want to push the guy out of shape," I said. "That's what it's all about," the third man shot back. "We've been pushing people out of shape for years. All it does is stretch 'em."

*

Seven, I'm not so sure. You are talking about pretty emotional stuff. You are talking about the sharing of feelings. That's only for women. They show their feelings more than men.

Baloney. Those first three letters above were from men. All the Bible quotes were from men. That's one of the troubles with our country. We leave the thinking to men and the feeling to women. It makes no sense. More to the point, it is dangerous. Cut a man off from his feelings and he is in trouble. He becomes a marvelous thinking machine and a wreck as a human being.

Recognizing this dangerous imbalance in our national life, our political parties, churches, corporations, and other institutions are at last elevating women to positions of responsibility.

*

Eight, O.K. But there are plenty of people who feel deeply without the church. Indeed, there are people outside the church who feel *more* deeply than people inside. "My best friend," you hear people say, "is a better Christian than I am and she never darkens the door of a church."

Of course. Eminently possible. But look at your friend closely. It is highly probable that, in 9 cases out of 10, he or she has experienced church somewhere. And not church broadly constructed as "love." But church narrowly constructed as "Where two or three are gathered in my name, there am I in the midst of them" (Matt. 18:20). Either that person had a direct experience of what we normally call church, or his parents made a church with him, or one or two other people did. And they did it because Jesus did it. They bore your friend's burden because they felt Jesus had somehow borne theirs.

Not true? Then keep going. Your friend may be a humanitarian, not because he was ever that close to anyone but because it is in his culture. But where did his culture come from? Straight out of the Hebrew-Christian tradition.

Or look at it another way. It may be your friend is not such a burden-bearer as you think. He may bear your burden and those of a few others like you. But again, what about people who are not like you? Is your friend limited or does his *koinonia* know no limits? If he is limited, then how "Christian" really is he? And if he is not limited, did he get that way without Jesus? If so, fine. *Any* means to reach that end.

It is here that I part company with Dallas and Explo '72. 80,000 young people turned on for Jesus. You can't beat that. But the sign that has been around for some time in the conservative Christian youth movement and was all over the national press from Dallas is the index finger pointing upward symbolizing "one way." That may be true for the Dallas youth. And it's beautiful if it is. But it may not be true for the two-thirds of the world that does not feel close to Jesus. You cannot tell a Jew like Einstein or a Buddhist like U Thant or an atheist like Bertrand Russell or a Hindu like Gandhi that there is only "one way" to the unlimited bearing of other people's burdens. That may be true for you. Say that. Say it with everything you have. But it may not be true for them. Say that too.

*

Nine, it always ends up here. The fact of the matter is that bearing one another's burdens *is* too much for us. *We* won't do it. It is too artificial. We don't want the communist student in our home for three weeks. We don't want the fellow fresh out of jail in our car every morning on our way to our work even though it may be the only way for him to get to *his* work. Like everything else in Christianity, bearing one another's burdens is completely unrealistic.

Precisely. *We* won't do it. We *can't* do it. It isn't in human nature to do it. That's the point. It is only in *divine* nature to do it. It is done through us, not by us. It has to be God because it *can't* be us. "God *is* love" (1 John 4:8). The church *are* the people who find themselves that close to people.

But isn't that semantic? Of course *we* do it. What's this "through you, not by you" stuff? It's we who are doing it.

But is it? That's what's unique about the church. It can claim *no* credit. "You did not choose me, but I chose you" (John 15:16). "This is *not* your own doing, it is the gift of God" (Eph. 2:8).

But is it? Isn't that semantic? Look, I'm extending my limits to the best of my ability. It's right, decent, proper, humanitarian, "liberal." Why bring *God* into it?

Because you will never extend your limits enough. You can't extend your limits enough. "That good that I would I do *not*" (Rom. 8:19). It's *beyond* your ability.

The church is in business to show us what is beyond our ability. To remind us that even though we have been to the moon and transplanted the heart, there are some things *we* cannot do. One of those things is to extend our limits to the point where we bear the burdens of other people. Therefore when we *do* bear other people's burdens it can't be us. It has to be God. Because *we* won't do it. We *can't* do it.

But couldn't you say the same thing about the signs of the zodiac? About Vishnu? Krishna? Buddha? The universal vibes?

Certainly. If they are indeed what get you to extend your limits. Someone once told me I was a Capricorn, and that Capricorns are nice. And I felt very extended. But how far *do* we extend with non-God motivators? Let's face it, in our culture we aren't motivated by Vishnu. We aren't motivated by Krishna. We aren't motivated by Buddha. And the things that do motivate us—like patriotism and avarice and self-fulfillment and altruism—never motivate us quite enough to get us really out there, really bearing the burden of the guy in North Vietnam or the gal in the church in Africa or the councilman in our city who won't vote for low-income housing.

If it isn't God that moves you to bear other people's burdens, what else could it be—*realistically?* Your parents? Your close friends? But we have already seen that in 9 cases out of 10 they were in turn motivated by the church. Your culture? But we have already seen that it too was motivated by the church.

I like the story that was played out in a church, to a church. A 17-year-old man stood up and said how he'd been through confirmation, done all the right things, thought all the right thoughts, said all the right words. But it wasn't until 2½ years later, not until he had felt the closeness of a small group of 8–10 church people, young and old, that he finally decided to join the church. The word he used was "love." And he said how very much he wanted now to be close to them, who had given him so much, who had shared so much, who had felt so much. And yes, he said how he wanted now to be close to the man on the cross behind the group, who had brought the group together. Because if he, the man, were responsible for that much love, then he, the young man, wanted to take his stand beside him, and be close, always close.

The church was empty. It was late at night. I was alone. But I bumped into each of the beautiful people. I thought of that young man. And how that is what we mean by church. And then I thought of the young couple. And how they had said, "We don't have anyone. Our folks are gone. If anything should happen to us, we want to leave our children to St. Luke." That's the church.

SEVEN

The Church Serves

I

The church serves. It was the first church's *diakonia*. It meant waiting on tables. It was a servant image. They extended it to giving food, drink, shelter, clothes, visiting the sick, the imprisoned (Matt. 25:-35–36).

It was "completely new."[1] It was a "radical change."[2] The leader is the servant.

> Whoever would be great among you must be your servant; and whoever would be first among you must be slave of all (Mark 10:43–44).

It was what made the church the church.

> The decisive point is that he sees in it the thing which makes a man his disciple.[3]

It was therefore the most important command.

> He demands love with an exclusiveness which means that *all* other commands lead up to it and *all* righteousness finds in it its norm.[4]

It was therefore the keystone of his plan. It had appeared nowhere else in ancient thought or action. It was a "full and resolute program."[5]

58

There are plenty of ways for a church to serve. Most, however, boil down to two. Everyone in a church has a major and a minor ministry, or "service," which is what the word "ministry" comes from. The major ministry is job and home. The minor ministry is some one service a person takes on because he or she is a "minister." It could be a task force to a nursing home. It could be running a political party. It could be working in a slum school. It could be going to school-board meetings.

Of course, the usual objection is: "Why do it through the church when I'm already doing it on my own through other groups—the political party, the Urban League, the Junior League, the Little League?"

But *are* you? *Will* you? A lot of us kid ourselves that we are "serving in the community" when we merely show up for an ice-cream social to preserve a historical site.

There are two kinds of service—social service and social action. Social service treats symptoms; social action treats causes. Social service is the Band-Aid; social action is the surgery. Social service takes a food basket to a needy family at Christmas; social action tries to eliminate the conditions which produce the hunger. Social service visits a man in a prison; social action reforms a penal system so primitive and barbarous its primary tool for correcting behavior is still punishment. Social service sends the Red Cross to Vietnam; social action uses every means at its disposal to end the Vietnam War.

Both social service *and* social action are necessary in churches. Often a person is not motivated to do anything about the penal system until he has visited a lonely young man in a jail cell. By the same token, a person may be motivated to do something about the prison system, but he may not know any prisoners. The church is in business to provide *both* social service *and* social action. A member can get aboard with either, but he must experience both.

But what if a member doesn't want either, let alone both? Then he can leave. He has to be given the message that loving his neighbor does not stop with loving his kids or the people next door. It never stops.

And the church is in business to tell him that. If it backs off at all it is not in business as a church.

But I gave at work. My company makes a profit. The government takes half. The government is in the business of social service. Therefore I have made my contribution. The same, of course, could be said of my taxes.

Nonsense. The government does not begin to get the job done. If it did, we wouldn't be in the mess we are. This kind of argument is usually nothing more than a rationalization to cover indolence. A person working 40 hours a week has 128 left. And he doesn't want anyone telling him how to spend them. But that is precisely what the church is in business to do. If he doesn't like it, then he need not join. If he's in and doesn't like it, he can leave.

This is also the heart of democracy. It is founded on a belief not only in the dignity of the common man but in his willingness to participate in community decision-making. That's a bold faith, but it's the point of America. And we know it. The Gallup Poll asked: "Would you accept service on a committee to deal with some local problem such as housing, recreation, traffic, health?" 59%, or a projected 69 million of us, said we would.[6]

II

One of the best ways to serve, to experience the corporate dimension of the first church's *diakonia* and *agape,* is to organize the middle class, which means organizing the church, the single largest organization of the middle class in America. It is a new way for the church in the 1970s. And, it could be argued, the church *must* go this or a similar way if it is ever going to make it out of the '70s with noticeably more impact than it made it into the '70s.

Such organizing springs from a monumental disenchantment with the system. There is the feeling that we are off course, that our values are crumbling. That the quality of our life is deteriorating. That our national priorities are askew.

People are upset by always higher taxes, impossible medical costs, the alienation of our youth, the pollution of our environment, highways through living rooms, racial injustice, our inability to extricate ourselves from Indochina.

Nobody asked us if we wanted our lakes polluted. Nobody asked us if we wanted our forests bulldozed. Nobody asked us if we wanted our incomes squandered. Nobody asked us if we wanted our young men killed in Vietnam.

There is the feeling of powerlessness. That we are no longer in control of our own destinies. That we are caught in a society nobody made and nobody wants. That the system is the enemy. That it is indifferent, dehumanized, out of control.

The average American is taxed $402.08 for arms. He is taxed $2.52 for food to feed his fellow citizens.[7]

75% of American Indian families have cash incomes of less than $3,000 a year.[8]

One out of three blacks is living in poverty.[9]

One out of every four persons 65 and over is living in poverty.[10]

13.4% of the country is *below* the poverty level.[11]

Half the poor have no medical insurance.[12]

56,000 are killed on the highways.[13]

Fifteen nations have higher literacy rates.[14]

Seventeen have lower infant mortality rates.[15]

There is the feeling that we do not control the system; the system controls us. That our cities are being strangled; our freedoms eroded; our creativity lost, our spirit killed.

Even those who are supposed to be in control are controlled. Our corporations are indifferent; our legislatures glacial; our community groups peripheral; our city councils treating symptoms not causes.

Even the people, which is in theory where the power is in a democracy, are powerless. They do not control the system, the system

controls them. Beyond a vote every two years the system is allowed
to go its own way. Stockholders' meetings last 12 minutes. Neither
manager nor politician is held accountable by the people.

It is our own fault. We have fled from our cities to live in a
microcosm of the kingdom of God where the major enemy is crab-
grass. We have moralized in our suburbs and rural communities while
our cities rot. We have gone our safe, antiseptic way in our golden
ghettos while others in our community do not have decent housing,
decent schools, decent food, decent jobs.

III

But that is only one side of the coin. The other side is that systems
can be changed; that they are changed by power; that power means
pressure; that pressure means people; and that people means us.

The word for "democracy" comes from the words for "power" and
"people." In a democracy the power is with the people. Only it isn't.
The people give the power up. It is the Achilles' heel of democracy.
We elect people to govern our destinies and then forget about those
destinies ourselves. Democracy may be the best government there is,
but it is flawed. The flaw is the people. The governed invariably leave
the government to the governors.

But it doesn't *have* to be that way. The system *can* be changed. It
will be changed by power. Power belongs to those who do the homework. And the homework in the 1970s is to organize. The name of
the game is to organize. We are de-humanized because we are dis-
organized. If we organize we can get the power to control the system
rather than be controlled by it. If we do not organize we will not get
the power to control the system and the system may go out of control
for good.

Let us not be worried about power. Power has been defined as the
capacity to make one's interests felt in community decision-making,
be that community a church or a school or a corporation or a family
or a bridge club or a city. The trouble is that the people's voice just
simply is not heard as often as it should be in community decision-

making. That is why your city council may not move with the speed
of light. That is why much that is done in your community may
appear to be simply shuffling deck chairs on the *Titanic.* That is why
we could fight a war half a world away that had never even been
declared by the people.

Power belongs to those who do the homework. The system is
dehumanized because we have not organized to humanize it. Don't
blame the politicians. Don't blame the executives. Don't blame the
labor leaders. Don't blame the school board or the principal.

We have no one to blame but ourselves. "We the people of the
United States." Only it hasn't been that way at all. It's been we the
individuals, each one doing his own thing and letting the whole thing
go to pot. It's been we the churches, each church doing its own thing.
It's been we the church members, each member doing his or her own
thing. And letting the whole thing become dehumanized. Neglecting
servanthood. Churches do not serve the communities in which they
exist. (And which serve *them,* incidentally, by giving them a whop-
ping tax break.)

IV

One way for churches to serve their communities is by replicating
such a community-organization model as the Greater Metropolitan
Federation of the Twin Cities.

The Federation is a power group. That is to say, like any group, it
seeks to bring people together to enable their opinion to be registered
in community decision-making.

How, then, is the Federation different from any other group?

For *one* thing, the Federation is big. It is composed of 125 community organizations. This means it is in communication with some
25,000 people.

For *another* thing, the Federation, unlike other groups, offers no
individual memberships. A person can only join as a member of an
organization. That is the point of power, of the corporate dimension
of *agape.* It is no longer enough in the 1970s to get even several

thousand individuals together. They must join *with the organization where they have their power.* That way their ability to be heard in community decision-making is enhanced dramatically.

A person can join, then, with nine of his friends whom he has organized to give himself a power base. Or he can join, as 78% have, as members of already existing organizations which have been in the community for years but have been relatively impotent in the giving of service. Like churches.

A *third* difference between the Federation and other groups is its newness. It is a new model for a new time. Community organization is an idea whose time has come. If you want to be in on the ground floor of such organizing, then the Federation model is for you in your city. To the best of my knowledge, this is one of the first attempts in the country to organize the middle class around its own concerns. The newness of it is exhilarating.

A *fourth* difference is the Federation's activism. It is in business for one reason only—action. Everything the Federation does is geared toward the one purpose of making its influence felt in community decision-making. The total program is to isolate issues, from taxation to education to penal reform, that are immediate, specific, realizable, actionable, and then to move on those issues dramatically and with dispatch.

For instance: we are in a housing crisis in the Twin Cities. There is no other word for it. Some 760,000 units must be built between now and the year 2000. 50,000 people, according to the Metropolitan Council, live in substandard housing in the metropolitan area. One-half of all American families, according to *Forbes* magazine, can afford to spend no more than $15,000 for a house. Less than one of every four families, according to the same magazine, can afford the average new house, priced at around $25,000.

That information is available. It can be read. It can be seen. The point is, what are we going to *do* about it? Are we going to do something in the area of low- and moderate-income housing or are we not? The Federation says that we are. The Federation wants its opinion registered. The Federation wants a voice in community decision-making. So the Federation puts 400 people into buses and descends on a housing hearing of the Metropolitan Council to show its support of the beleagured Housing Development Guide. It was far and away the largest number of people ever to show up for a Metro Council hearing.

However, that was not enough. Everybody is for people living in houses. It was not enough to support such God, motherhood, and apple pie. The issue, the heart of the matter, was Policy 14 and who was going to support that. It reads: "Assign a lower priority in the review of federal fund requests to municipalities whose plans and ordinances do not provide for low- and moderate-income housing." We showed up, 80% of us from the suburbs, to support that. It was an issue. It was immediate, specific, realizable, and actionable. We moved, dramatically and with dispatch, to register our opinion in community decision-making. And we prevailed. Policy 14 remains. The church *organized* its love. It *served* its community.

A *fifth* difference, then, between the Federation and other groups, is that the Federation is going to make enemies. We were vigorously opposed in the hearing by the League of Municipalities. There were some very uptight people in that room that night. And that's all right. It's the name of the game. They have a right to do their thing just as we have a right to do ours. The point is that the victory is going to go to the group that is organized. Of 48 speakers that night, 36 were from the Federation. Of 450 people in that room, 400 were from the Federation. Now, obviously, numbers aren't everything, but they are something, and in the organization game, if you don't have the money you have to have the numbers, and they count for a lot, as any community decision-maker called a politician will tell you.

Sixth, it is apparent, then, that the Federation, unlike many groups, has to be tight, disciplined, organized, if it is going to be structured for action. It is. There is a rigid system of accountability which you just don't find in most volunteer organizations. Everyone has a job description. Decisions are made by the 125-member Action Council

plus the 14 officers. There is a full-time staff of two. Each Action
Council Representative reports to an Area Vice President. Each Area
Vice President reports to the President. Each Action Council Representative is responsible for seeing that every member of his or her
group is involved in an Action Campaign, a Coalition Action, or a
Research Action. Each Area Vice President is responsible for seeing
that each Action Council Representative secures the involvement of
each member of his or her group. If people do not want to be so
involved, then there is no point in their being in the Federation.
Believe me, they know it. That's why they're in it.

Seventh, the Federation, unlike some groups, does not try to cover
the waterfront. At one time the full resources of the Federation were
behind only seven issues:

Moderate-income housing in a major utility's private development;

Nuclear safety, exorbitant rates, and the need for state control
of another major utility;

Transit rather than concrete for a projected new interstate;

Extension of medical care to all and at reasonable costs;

Extension of basic civil liberties to high school students;

Extension of credit to women;

Extension of justice to inmates of prisons.

Now, it is important to remember that not everyone in the Federation will agree with all the Federation's campaigns. The seven mentioned above *have* been voted by the Federation's Action Council. But
that does not mean that every member of every one of the 125 Federation organizations will agree with all the campaigns. Nor does it mean
that every member of every organization must participate in every one
of the campaigns. That is not the point of the Federation.

The point of the Federation is to put enough people together at
enough times to apply enough pressure to accomplish some basic

reordering of community priorities. The Federation is a bold new vehicle for getting that agreement registered with those human beings who make the priority decisions in our community. It is a people's lobby.

To summarize: the goal is to serve the community. It is to "seek justice" (Isa. 1:18). It is to make democracy work. It is to humanize the system. It is to give people a chance to be heard in community decision-making. One means of reaching that goal is to organize large groups of middle-class people to move dramatically and with dispatch on issues that are immediate, specific, realizable, and actionable. We do so through a disciplined system of accountability. And we have fun.

V

Now there are those, of course, who do not agree that this is the way for churches to organize for creative social change.

The *first* objection is that we are operating outside the system. If you want to do this sort of thing, the objection goes, do it through the political parties. That is what they are for. Don't waste everybody's time by creating, in effect, a third political party.

This, of course, would be lovely if it worked. Unfortunately it doesn't. The two political parties do not begin to reach the people. According to a University of Michigan study: only 8% of the people ever attend political meetings; only 7% ever give money to a campaign; only 5% actually belong to a political club or other organization; and only 3% do any other type of work for candidate or party.[16]

Put another way, James Reston quotes John Gardner as saying:

> 65% of the eligible do not vote regularly; half of them cannot name their congressman; 65% cannot name both of their senators; 85% are not able to identify anything their congressman has done; 96% cannot identify any policy their congressman stands for.[17]

In other words, which is no news, the political parties just are not where the action is for the vast majority of Americans.

Nor are they necessarily where the action should be. There is nothing sacred about the two parties. They are not even mentioned in the *Federalist Papers*. The multiplicity of factions, however, is. It was what Madison called "the great variety of interests, parties, and sects" in *Federalist 51* that would prevent the establishment of a tyrannous majority and allow democracy to work.

It is also the height of realism to realize that certain problems are not necessarily amenable to political solution. We have politicians from both parties, for instance, beginning with the great conservative Robert Taft, loudly proclaiming allegiance to fair housing, open housing, low- and moderate-income housing, even passing laws to establish such housing, but then it all comes down to whether or not a major utility is going to include such housing in its 1,000-acre development. Neither political party either has or would have the slightest effect on the utility's will in this matter. Organized bipartisan citizen pressure, however, does have an effect. It is one way to put "Love your neighbor" into *action*. You *organize* your love. The way the Good Samaritan organized his. That makes it count.

As to the objection that middle-class organizing means founding a new political party, that is, of course, erroneous. Many middle-class people are already active in their respective parties. They have no thought whatever of forming another party. Such thoughts are historically naive as well as politically inept. What churches are doing is working within the system to make the system work. And that means applying the right pressure at the right time on the right people to insure that not only government but education, business, labor, the church itself, and all our social institutions become pervious at last to the popular will. *Any* means to register that will should be encouraged in a democracy. Indeed, that is the point of democracy: to give as many people as possible a voice in community decision-making, some control over their own destinies, and thus, at last, some humanity to their tragically dehumanized system.

*

A *second* objection is that the Federation is too aggressive. It has a tendency to leap before it looks. It makes a lot of noise, like the 400 people, but where are its 50-page position papers? Where are all the facts on both sides of its issues? What right does it have to move when it doesn't have all the facts?

Surely this is one of the great copouts of all time and the middle-class copout par excellence. As we have seen, many middle-class people feel they can't move until they have all the facts. But since they will never have all the facts they will never move. And that is precisely the reason we are in the malaise we are in, in this country. We have taken the route of the intellectual copout. We have not moved. We have researched everything to death. And we are now in great trouble with the air we breathe, the water we drink, the food we eat, the things we buy, the wars we fight.

The fact of the matter is that on most of the major issues before the country the position papers have been written by such organizations as the local Citizens League, the League of Women Voters, the Urban Coalition, Common Cause, the political parties, the special interest groups on both sides. We have the facts. That is not the issue. The issue is that we do not have the will. We are paralyzed. We know it but we will not do it because we do not feel it. How is a person making $20,000 a year and living in a $50,000 house going to *feel* anything about the one making $5,000 a year and living in a hovel? It's hard. But the amazing thing is that it's happening. And that's why the Federation is the size that it is. Church people do care. It is less hard, of course, to feel about taxes and education and the pollution of your suburban lake. That kind of *self*-interest is also why the Federation is as large as it is.

Another form of the aggressive objection is that the Federation, because its tactics are highly visible, is not interested in results. It is not serious. All it wants to do is make a play for the media and gorge its appetite for power.

Such an objection imputes low motives and is to be rejected out of hand.

*

A final form of the aggressive objection is that, as we have seen, while I agree with your ends, I disagree with your means. You are too aggressive, too pushy, too noisy, too visible. You put women in hard-hats on the downtown mall and next morning have a lead editorial in the paper. You are letting the end justify the means.

Like so many shibboleths, this one relieves us of the need to think. On the one hand, we are not that aggressive. We are not violent. We do not break the law. On the other hand, we, like everyone else, choose the means appropriate to our end. The end of independence, for instance, the late Saul Alinsky pointed out, justified the grossly distorted Declaration of Independence. Talk about having all the facts, there was nothing in the Declaration about the food from England for the colonies in times of famine, nothing about the medicines from England in times of disease, nothing about the troops from England to fight the Indians. Nor should there have been. The end of getting men to fight apparently justified the means of not telling them all the truth. One need not be an expert at extrapolation to infer the same ends-means game being played over the Indochina war, and being played, too, I might add, by the corporation, the school board, the PTA, and the church.

"The means," Hamilton wrote in *Federalist 23,* "ought to be pro-portioned to the end."

> What is a power [he asked in *33*] but the ability or faculty of doing a thing? What is the ability to do a thing, but the power of employing the *means* [italics his] necessary to its execution?

Or, as we have seen his counterpart, Madison, putting it in *Federalist 44:*

> No axiom is more clearly established in law, or in reason, than that wherever the end is required, the means are authorized.

Lincoln, the defender of freedom, Alinsky reminded us, suspends habeas corpus. Sam Adams, the defender of revolution, opposes

Shays's Rebellion. Gandhi, the defender of nonviolence, says nothing when Nehru goes to war against Pakistan over Kashmir. Eight months after securing their independence by nonviolence, the Indian National Congress outlaws passive resistance. A local bank officer leads the fight for a strong Jaycee resolution against a local polluter. He forgets that his bank has a large interest in the polluter. Bank officials immediately call all the people they know on the resolutions committee to rescind their resolution. Nobody's skirts are clean in the ends-means game. We all choose means that work to reach our ends. If questioned, we justify those means by moralizing.

*

A *third* objection to the Federation is that it is too middle class. There are not many black faces in the Federation. There are not many Indians. There are not many poor.

That, of course, is precisely the *point* of the Federation. The time has come for us to get our own thing together so that we can help the poor, the black, the Indian with their thing. If the old way of colonialism had worked, that would be one thing. But it has patently not worked. The old jumping-in-the-station-wagon-and-roaring-off-to-the-reservation bit is over. The time has come to apply massive pressure to one of the most atavistic institutions in America, the B.I.A. (Bureau of Indian Affairs).

Like it or not, the middle class is where it is at in this country. The great middle is where the great power is. We are a country of the middle class. It is a political truism that no enduring social change is going to happen in this country unless it happens through the middle class. John Gardner knows this, which is why he started Common Cause, and before that the Urban Coalition. James Reston knows it. All you have to do is read him. And most assuredly every politician in the country knows it, from Mr. Nixon to Bobby Seale.

*

Which leads to a *fourth* objection, that the Federation is too suburban. 65% of our organizations come from the suburbs.

Upon reflection, the logic is inescapable. If the middle class is where it is at in this country, the suburbs are where the middle class is. For the first time in history, the balance of power in the country has shifted from the cities to the suburbs. According to the 1970 Census, more people live now in suburbs than in cities or rural communities. Organize the suburbs, then, and you are on your way to organizing the country. We are turning the silent majority into the vocal majority.

*

Which leads to a *fifth* objection, that the Federation is too churchy. 60% of our organizations come from churches or church-related groups.

Again the logic is inescapable. If the middle class is where it's at, and if the suburbs are where the middle class is, *the one organization that reaches the most middle-class people is, like it or not, the church.* No other organization is in touch with so many people in this country. 5% belong to political parties. 63% belong to church and synagogue. That's 130 million people. No other organization comes anywhere near reaching that many people. Two-thirds of every community belong to that community's religious institutions. Two-thirds of every school board, two-thirds of every city council, two-thirds of every legislature, two-thirds of every board of directors, two-thirds of every labor union are already in the churches. In many cases, it is virtually 100%. Turn on the church, then, and you could turn on the country.

There are those, of course, who argue that the church has no business getting involved in this sort of thing. The most the church can do is remind people to get active on their own, in the political or civic group of their choice. The argument is Biblically illiterate.

> I hate, I despise your feasts [the prophet said],
> and I take no delight in your solemn assemblies. . . .
> Take away from me the noise of your songs;
> to the melody of your harps I will not listen.
> But let justice roll down like waters, and righteousness like an
> ever-flowing stream (Amos 5: 21, 23–24).

It is *precisely* the job of the church to seek justice. To be a church *is* to seek justice. The *point* of religion is low-income housing in the suburbs. How else can a man spell out the injunction of his religion to love his neighbor? The *point* of religion is what happens in prisons. How else can we respond to Christ's "I was in prison and you came to me"? (Matt. 25:36) The question is not what right does the church have to speak, but what right does the church have to be silent?

*

A *sixth* objection is that Federation members are too liberal. They come from only one end of the political spectrum.

That is not true. Members of both parties and members of neither party are in the Federation.

These are not liberal or conservative issues. We have to jettison that kind of thinking. They are human issues and several thousand human beings are going to solve them. What is liberal or conservative about a four-lane highway through the heart of a lake area? What is liberal or conservative about a bill of rights in 1973 America for high school students? "We are all Republicans," Jefferson said. "We are all Federalist."[18] And maybe a little more of that kind of thinking and feeling and acting and a little less of the partisan kind might help us all.

*

A *seventh* objection to the Federation is that we will never be able to organize the very people we are trying to organize. It is one thing to organize the blacks of Birmingham. It is another thing to organize the whites of the suburbs. You can organize only where there have been specific and long-standing grievances. In a word, you can organize the have-nots, but you cannot organize the haves.

That may be true. But so far it is false. The haves are organizing and they are organizing fast. One reason is that we are all in this together. One man's pollution is another's. The specific and long-standing grievances have at last become the specific and long-standing grievances of the middle class. It is the ecological crisis that has done it. For the first time in the history of the country, it is in the self-interest of the middle class to get itself together to begin to assure sheer physical survival. A polluted river through a suburb is a microcosm of self-interest around which the middle class is moved to organize.

*

A *final* objection to the Federation is that it is too democratic. It is the old power-to-the people bit which the founders of our country specifically eschewed. They went for a republic instead. Consequently in the Federation you get a bunch of do-gooders who want to do their thing but have neither the time, the money, nor the expertise with which to do it. Better to leave this kind of thing to the established community decision-makers rather than roil the waters with the nonestablished.

Again, this would be fine if it worked. But it hasn't. It is the old argument about leaving war to the generals. But it hasn't worked. It has just meant leaving pollution to the polluters, television to the FCC, churches to the clerics, corporations to the directors, schools to the school boards, prisons to the wardens, politics to the politicians.

It is time to be more democratic and less republican, both without capital letters. It is time to give more power to the people and less to their leaders. It is time, in other words, for the average person to take more of a say in the control of his destiny. It is time, in one word, to organize.

Bad policies are made by good people who don't speak up. The oldest citizenship game in the world is decision by default. Again, it is the Achilles' heel of democracy. Or, as the great conservative Edmund Burke put it: "The only thing necessary for evil to triumph is for enough good men to do nothing."

The time is ripe to do much—to get ourselves back on course, shore up our crumbling values, ameliorate the quality of our life, set our national and local priorities in cement.

> We have long entertained a wonderfully complacent notion [says historian Thomas Fleming] that if each of us minds his own business, well, the system will take care of itself. It *isn't* taking care of itself.

Thus we're going to have to do something we haven't done since the late 18th century, when a lawyer named Jefferson, a planter named Washington, a printer named Franklin, a banker named Morris—and others of varied occupations—made themselves experts in statecraft in order to found a new nation.

So, today, must a lot of us—on a local, grassroots, community level —begin to think hard about how our nation can be made to work. We're badly out of practice. But we had better start.[19]

One way to start is to organize *your* church for social service and social action.

EIGHT

How to Answer Objections to Planning

Now there are, of course, objections to planning. Here's how they run.

I

First objection. If you go for management by objectives—such as the Suffering Servant and study, share, serve—you are simply being mesmerized by one more fad of American capitalism.

That may be. But it is a fad that works. Any way you slice it, American capitalism is one of the more ingenious systems devised by the mind of man. It works. And, much as we deplore it, when only 5% of the world's population enjoys 40% of its wealth, it works very well indeed.

But deracinate it from capitalism. That is not the point. The point is that *any* enterprise (1) sets a goal, (2) determines the means for reaching the goal, (3) lays out dates and personnel. A girl wants to be a lawyer (that's goal). She takes certain courses (that's means). She decides on a certain time period and whether or not she can sustain both a profession and a marriage (that's dates and personnel).

In other words, it is not a matter of being euchred once more by the American free-enterprise system. It is a matter of *doing what you have done all along in every other area of your life.* If you don't want to call it planning, call it "doing what you've always done."

The point is to do it in the *church* as well as in the job, the family, the Little League, the fishing trip. Why? Because it works. And you know it works because that is the way you live. Be consistent. Don't shortchange the church. If you were shipwrecked on a desert island, by the third day you would be planning. Who gets the coconuts? Who washes the old coconuts? Even the way your mother made peanut butter sandwiches was planned.

II

Second objection to adopting a plan. Many people won't like it.

Of course they won't like it. Some people like Wheaties. Others like Cheerios. You go to one service station because it has Pennzoil. You go to another because it has Union Oil.

Why is it always necessary for *churches* to keep *everyone* happy? That makes as much sense as saying the local Ford dealer should also sell Cadillacs, Jeeps, Toyotas, and Boeing 747s.

It is also historically silly. The reason we have Catholics and Protestants is that you *can't* keep everyone happy. The reason we have different churches of the *same* denomination in the *same* town is again, you can't keep everyone happy. Nor should you. Peter did it his way. Paul did it his. They were not happy with each other. But both won people for Christ.

But what if every church did this? Wouldn't there be a lot of people without a church?

No. They would have theirs. For one thing, every church won't do this. For another, all they would need to do if every church did it, would be to put their own group together. If you didn't want to belong to any of the "planned" churches in a community, you could start an "unplanned" one. However, you can't, of course, start anything without a plan. So you're already planning. There will always be a plan even for those who don't like to plan.

But isn't the church supposed to be be the great reconciler? "God was in Christ reconciling the world to himself" (2 Cor. 5:19). You don't kick people out of families just because they don't buy the family plan. You love them. You take them back, as the Prodigal Son. It was a gospel of reconciliation.

Certainly it was. But that never meant there would not be division. You had to choose. Did you *want* to be reconciled or not? The Prodigal Son did. And the prodigal father was willing to let him go until he did.

> Choose this day whom you will serve (Josh. 24:15).

> I have not come to bring peace, but a sword. . . . I have come to set a man against his father, and a daughter against her mother . . . (Matt. 10:34–35).

Of course the church reconciles. But it does not reconcile to the point of watering down. That's why Jesus, the incarnation of love, could talk so honestly about hate.

> If any one comes to me and does not hate his own father and mother and wife and children and brothers and sisters, yes, even his own life, he cannot be my disciple (Luke 14:26).

The church reconciles, yes. But often it does so by division. Better a divided church that stands for something than a united church that stands for nothing. Or that falls for everything.

III

Third objection. So how is buying the plan any different from buying a theology? All you have is a new fundamentalism of action replacing the old fundamentalism of faith. And all the strictures of rigidity, exclusivism, pharisaism and much else urged against the old "fundamentals" can be urged against the new "fundamentals" of study, share, and serve.

Fair enough. It *is* a new fundamentalism. But with the radical difference that it's not what you believe but what you *do* that counts. If you want to join the organization of the Suffering Servant but don't want to *do* any suffering service, then you'd better not join. That is precisely the point of using *this* style to organize the church for action.

And it's some style. Read Dean Kelley's *Why Conservative Churches are Growing* (published by Harper & Row). They are growing because they *require* certain beliefs of their members. Now, if they would only require certain *actions,* they would be hot churches. The trouble is you can walk into any conservative church in America, say you've been "washed in the blood of the lamb," say all the "right things," and then turn around and zap the guy next door because he's black or because he lives in North Vietnam. Of course, this is true not only of conservative churches but of liberal ones as well.

No ethical means test is ever administered to church members. Only an intellectual means test. "Do you accept Christ as your personal Savior?" All you have to do is say Yes and then zap. Ah, but who would administer the ethical means test? The same person who administers the intellectual one, namely, the minister. He asks people before they join if they buy the *kerygma,* the *koinonia,* and the *diakonia.* If they don't, then they don't join. If they do, then they do join and they're off.

Broadly speaking, of course, any enterprise can be "accused" (if you're a liberal it's always a pejorative) of fundamentalism. Any corporation has its "fundamental policy objectives." If you don't like them you don't work for them. It's just that simple. Any game has its fundamental rules. If you want to run from home to first by way of third, you're in the wrong ballgame. Certainly most families have their fundamentals. Bed at a certain time. Up at a certain time. Grace before meals. Lock the doors. Go to college. Vote in each election. Consequently, if one faults a system for being "fundamentalist," one should realize that one is faulting oneself as well for being equally fundamentalist.

IV

Fourth objection. O.K. So we're running a church not a business. We're not in this for profits. We're in it for God.

The objection is semantic. Certainly God wants a church to be "profitable." He wants it to produce more and better Christians. That is its *job* as a church (Matt. 28:19), just as Snocat's *job* as a manufacturer is to produce more and better snowmobiles.

Certainly church members also want churches to be "profitable." A church member who works for an insurance company will want his church to collect on pledges just the way he collects on premiums. No premium—no insurance. It is the same with the banker. No mortgage payment—no mortgage. Therefore it is the same with the church. No pledge—no church membership. You can't have it both ways. You can't operate on a double standard. Why should a man's standards be high for his business and invariably low for his church? That's the point. They shouldn't.

But the objection goes deeper than this. There is an implicit disparagement of "business." When we say we don't want our churches run like businesses, we are saying that we don't want people treated as "cogs" for the sake of "efficiency." Agreed. But, *(a)*, that is not the way businesses need to be run, and many would argue it is not the way they *are* run. Profit and people go together. You can't have the one without the other. Therefore the happier you make people the more you make profit. And every firm has its stories about the people they hired from jail, the alcoholics they have stuck with, the man they did not transfer because it would be too hard on his family.

(b) It is precisely my contention that churches *should* be run more like businesses and less like churches. That will make each of them *more* of a church. Efficiency does not mean depersonalization. It means getting the job done. Jesus, by that definition, was "efficient." He got the job done. He *was* the Suffering Servant. *Anything* goes in churches to get people to be suffering servants too. But anything will often *not* go if it is not *planned* to go. "Discoveries," it has been said, "are prepared accidents." The point being that such accidents rarely happen to the unprepared, the un-planned. "Chance," said Pasteur, "favors the prepared mind." Inventing, Edison said, is 99% perspiration and 1% inspiration. Again, the point is that the inspired have perspired. They have done the homework necessary to invent.

No, this does not mean you cannot have unprepared accidents.

"The wind blows where it wills" (John 3:8). You can't restrict the Spirit to *any* system. It only means that *more* "accidents" come to the prepared than to the unprepared. Remember: even your own conversion was prepared by someone. It was also prepared by you. You *went* to the confirmation class or the evangelist's tent or the church. Or you read the Bible, prayed, visited in a jail. The disciples were with Jesus 3 years. *Then* the Spirit struck.

(c) Having said this, however, a caveat is in order. Just as the danger of running a church "like a church" is do-nothing softness, so the danger of running a church "like a business" is do-everything hardness. My contention is that we've given the "soft" way a chance in America, and that it has patently failed. However, in giving the "hard" way a chance to succeed it must be remembered that a church that is hard on planning must be soft on people. It must bend over backwards to show how much it loves them. This means an abundance of small groups. It means emotional services of worship. It means a great deal of calling in homes. Knowing this, and doing it, a hard church should become even softer than a soft church.

V

A *fifth* objection to planning is that it's closed. An in-group comes up with the plan, and that's it.

But that's not it. In the first place, the planning process has been open to the entire congregation. Therefore, if you did not participate you have no one to blame but yourself.

In the second place, the plan is always open-ended. That is to say, at the end of all the offerings, in each of the 3 areas, it is left blank. It may be that what is offered doesn't click with a member and he or she can come up with something better. If so, fine. That can be "negotiated." What cannot be negotiated is that *something* be done in each of the 3 areas—study, share, serve.

It is presumptuous of a church to feel it has all the implementations of planning within its four walls. For instance, a busy executive may be far better off spending his "study" time teaching his own children from the Bible at home rather than teaching someone else's children at church. Fine. Let him teach his children. The point is he is doing something in area No. 1, Study.

VI

Sixth objection. Church planning stifles the Spirit.

On the contrary. It *releases* the Spirit. It opens people *to* the Spirit. It *counts* on the Spirit. There is nothing inherent in structure which is antithetical to Spirit. The free Christian, Luther pointed out, is "slave of all." The point of suffering service is that it frees people to be what they were meant to be. Jesus was so free he could voluntarily die. Structure is to the Spirit what tracks are to a train. A restriction that gives freedom.

Spirit *follows* structure. Not always, obviously. But often. *Most* often. Even the Holy Rollers have to get the people into the tent. That's structure. Even Billy Graham "winds them up with singing." That's structure. Isaiah was in a worship service when the Spirit struck (Isa. 6). Structure. The disciples added another person to their ranks. Structure. They stayed together. Structure. They were in a room. Structure. *Then* the Holy Spirit struck (Acts 2:1).

The point is not structure vs. no structure but which structure are you going to choose? How is the Spirit going to be released for you? Presumably you will belong to the church whose structure *best* releases the Spirit for you. The church *will* be structured *to* release the Spirit. That is its *raison d'être* as a church. One structure is Study-Share-Serve. If it turns you on, fine. If it doesn't, equally fine. Just find a structure which does. Or devise your own.

Because the Spirit is what it's all about. You are in the church to get the Spirit. More accurately: you are in the church to let the Spirit get you.

VII

Seventh objection. Isn't this heresy? All you have done has been to take one part of the Bible and emphasize it.

Of course. That's what a heresy is. It is an overemphasis on one side of the truth. Luther was a heretic. He overemphasized faith. Paul was a heretic. He overemphasized grace. Jesus was a heretic. He overemphasized the Suffering Servant. It's all a matter of which heresy you're going to choose. Orthodoxy is what I believe; heresy is what you believe. One person's heresy is another person's orthodoxy.

Let's pit heresies. My contention is that the American church has overemphasized the "soft" side of Jesus for years. "He walks with me and he talks with me." Personal evangelism. Personal salvation. And so on. All very fine, make no mistake. But not fine enough.

It is time for a new heresy to balance the old one. Namely, the heresy of overemphasizing in the 1970s the "hard" side of Jesus. Deny yourself. Take up your cross. Follow me. Feed the hungry. Clothe the naked. Care for the sick. Visit the jailed. Free the oppressed. *Be* a suffering servant. If you don't want that heresy, then go to another church. But remember, you will not be a Christian until you get that heresy. More to the point: until it gets you.

NINE

How to Organize Your Minister

I

The minister's job is to plan. It is much else, of course, but it is this first. Most ministers come to churches without a plan in their heads for how they are going to *run* the church. Worse yet, after 1, 3, 5 years on the job they still don't have a plan.

The trouble is with the seminaries. The ministers were never trained how to plan. In most seminaries there is nothing even remotely resembling a planning course. Our business schools train people to be businessmen (and women). Our seminaries train people to be nice guys (and gals).

The trouble is also, of course, with the ministers themselves. They have sinecures and don't need to plan.

There are three parts to planning. Think, think, and think. The only way to plan is to glue the seat of the pants to the seat of the chair. The trouble is that most ministers are as lazy as anybody else. They haven't done any real *thinking* since their last exam in Greek (which subject, don't kid yourself, most do not take).

To get a minister to plan, you have to get him to a planner. The breed is in any large city and should be in any large seminary. The church should be willing to pay if necessary to have their minister take a planning course either from a local consultant firm or from a local college or university, or as an extension course, or at a seminary. Such a course should be a *condition* of every call. Since calls are reviewed by congregations every year, this catches both the minister coming to a church *and* the minister already in a church.

Planning takes time. Specifically, it takes 1–2 years to write and disseminate a plan. It takes another 1–2 years to begin to implement it. This means a maximum of two years in small churches to get under way. It means a maximum of four years in large churches. A small church is up to 300 members, which most are. A large church is 2,000 members or more.

The surest way for a minister to get into trouble is to come into a church and try to superimpose an entire plan at once. It can't be done. Now, as we have seen above, he may have the outline of such a plan in mind from his previous jobs, his Bible, his prayer, his experience of the Spirit. He will certainly have the goal, suffering service. But if he comes into a church and doesn't listen to where the people are, he is not likely to get them where he wants them to be.

In this sense, different from the sense used earlier, it is the opposite of presidential politics. The new president tries to sell his whole package to Congress in "the first 100 days." It's when he has the mandate of the people and the most clout. It is invariably gone or diminished by the off-year elections two years hence.

In the church, however, the first 100 days and often the first two years are the time when the minister has least clout. He is being looked over. His sermons are being sampled. They are getting to know him as a person. Not until then is the trust level sufficiently high for the church to move.

II

The minister is the key to planning, since he is the one you hire to plan.

The key to the minister, then, is obviously to get a good one. Correction: an excellent one. And the key to getting an excellent one is to organize.

Step 1. Pack the nominating committee. Somebody always packs it, and the key is *who. You* be the packer. Draw up a slate of your twelve (or whatever your denomination's rules call for) and have it introduced by the chairman (it's always a man) of the pastoral nominating committee. Either you be the chairman or have one of your close friends chairman. Failing that, you will either have to persuade the chairman or pull a love play. A love play would be inviting the chairman to your house to meet with 20 of your friends. Failing *that,* you will simply have to get a majority out to the congregational meeting who will be your supporters.

But support what? Support the election of a pastoral nominating committee in which the *majority* want your church to be a suffering servant. Not everyone, note; simply a majority. Obviously everyone doesn't want your church to be a suffering servant or you would be one already. You'd better start working on your differences now. In *this* committee. It is *the* most important committee ever formed in a church. And it is almost always formed in the wrong way. Either the departing minister packs it with his buddies or the official board with theirs. But these people may have *nothing* to do with a style of suffering service. Indeed, they *don't* have anything to do with it or your church would be a suffering servant under their leadership. But it isn't. Therefore *you* be the packer.

Be sure, of course, that half the committee are women and that 1/6 are under 18, 1/6 18–25, 1/6 25–35. In many congregations more than half the people, if you include all the children, are under 35. After all, it is as much their church as anyone else's. Indeed it could be agreed it is *more* their church: in the next 10, 20, 30 years the older people will be gone.

*

Step 2. Insist on the following conditions:

(a) That the person you call spend four hours a day, five days a week, planning. Preferably in one chunk—morning, afternoon, or night. That this time consist, in large part, of sermon preparation, since it is in the sermons that the strategic or overall plan is presented

and re-presented. That this time *not* be spent on tactical or operational planning. You have purchased the services of a man or woman to *think*. His primary job is, as general manager of your operation, to provide the *goals*. His *secondary* job is to provide the *means* of reaching those goals. Most institutions go off the track most often because the No. 1 person doesn't plan. He is too busy executing. He doesn't glue the seat of the pants to the seat of the chair and think about what his organization should *be*.

(b) Insist that the person you hire be tough on money. If he doesn't like to "raise money," stay away from him. If he leaves the money raising to "the men of the church," he's not your man. If he "doesn't want to see what people give," then you don't want to see what he can give you. It won't be much.

Close to the heart of any enterprise is the money raised to keep it afloat. Jesus never backed off money-talk. Twenty of his thirty parables are on stewardship. Paul praised good giving (2 Cor. 8:1f.; 9: 6f.). Any minister who is "too busy" to raise money is too busy to be a minister. Any minister who says, "What a man gives is between him and God" is simply washing his hands of the man. Not all of the man, to be sure. But enough of the man to make a difference. It is precisely this attitude on the part of ministers that is responsible in large part for the abysmal giving in Protestant churches. The average Protestant gives a stunning $89.12 a year to his church. That works out to two dimes and four pennies a day.

(c) Insist on looking at his track record. What has he organized? Even if he is fresh out of seminary, find out *specifically* and in *detail what* he has *organized*. More to the point: whom he has organized. Organization is simply a lot of people doing one thing at one time and then following through. If your man has been in parishes for 10 years and *none* of those parishes has increased its benevolences significantly, let alone gotten them up to 1:1, then you don't want him running your show. It's just that simple.

(d) Don't read his letters of recommendation. They're obviously written by his friends. Find out if he has any enemies. If he doesn't,

you don't want him. It proves he's a namby-pamby leader. Get the names of the people who *left* his church. Find out why. If they left, and left in large numbers, because he was trying to get the church to be a suffering servant, then you may have one of the hottest articles ever to come down the ministerial pike.

Ask the mayor if he has ever heard of the man. Ask the editor of the local paper. Ask the chairman of his political party. Ask any gas-station attendant within a 2-mile radius of the church if he has ever heard of the church.

(e) Ask him what his work hours are. If he hasn't been giving his present church at *least* 72 hours a week, then you don't want him. The Christian enterprise is a big, tough, demanding job, and if he isn't used to working long, hard hours, don't dally with him. After all, over a six-day week, that's only 12 hours a day. If he arrives at work at 8:00 and stays until 6:00, that's 10 hours right there. Two more hours for evening meetings and you have your 12. If he can't hack that minimal amount of time out of a 119-waking-hour week (7 hours a night for sleep), then you don't want him running your show. After all, 119 − 72 leaves 47 *free* hours a week, which is almost exactly two entire *days* off.

*

Step 3. If all the above fails, and you find you are not attracting a top minister, *go it on your own without a minister.* Don't throw in the sponge and water down your expectations. It may take 6 months. It may take a year. It may even take two years. But if you hold fast to the standards of suffering service, your man will come to you. He will be drawn like a filing to a magnet. The profession *knows* where the hot churches are. Furthermore, while you wait you have the advantage of losing members. All the peripherals will drop off like flies because they don't like "going to a church without a minister." In other words, you will already have done one of your minister's first jobs for him long before he even arrives on the scene. You will have a trimmed-down membership ready to *go.*

Of course, this kind of thing works both ways. If a committee is not asking these kinds of questions, a minister had better watch out getting involved with them. If they don't have a representative committee, he'd better watch out. And so on.

III

But what if you *have* a minister? And he has *no* plans for leaving? And he is *not* excellent?

Again you must organize. You have five options:

Option 1. Work with him. Obviously this is the best. The whole team is pulling together. You and your people may very well find that your minister has been looking for you all along. He will welcome you with open arms. Most ministers are like anyone else: they don't want to get too far out on a limb without looking back to see who's behind them. Where have you *been?* But the important thing is that you're here. Now. You can move. Together.

Step 1. Call your minister for an appointment. Tell him when you get there that you've drawn up a tactical plan for the church to become a suffering servant. Show him the plan in Chapter 3. Or show him one more specifically tailored to your situation. Just be sure it covers the *kerygma,* the *koinonia,* and the *diakonia.* Tell him you and some of your friends are most enthusiastic about working with him on it. Tell him each of you has pledged five hours a week. (Since you have eight people that is 40 "man" hours, the equivalent of a new staff person at the church. He will be impressed.) Tell him you're sure he has a plan, too, either written or in his head. You'd like to leave your plan with him (keeping a carbon, of course) and then get together with him again in two weeks, same time, same place if that's convenient, *so you can see his plan.* At this point you make very clear that *he* is the planner, not you. You are not pushing your plan. You are pushing him to plan. You want him to do it so his ego will be involved. Certainly you don't need yours involved, since you get your ego trips at your job.

Check point. If it has to be your plan, you have failed the first test of organizing, which is a submerged ego. Better look at yourself carefully. Do not go to the minister if the plan you lay on him has to be yours. You are an egoist, not an organizer. "He emptied himself, taking the form of a slave" (Phil. 2:7). And organized the world.

Step 2. Your next meeting with the minister. Is he receptive? Has he thought it through? Has he *written* the plan? Put it into his words? Taken the best from yours and his?

If he has, then you're on your way. Ask him how you can be helpful in getting the official board to adopt the plan. Work *with* him, in other words, to draw up a plan for getting the servanthood plan thoroughly aired, debated, codified, adopted. At the same time, tell him you have some people ready to begin to work the plan now. Tonight. You want him to come to a meeting at your house to meet with you and your seven friends. Together you will begin to be suffering servants. You will be his support group. You will work the plan while the official board works *on* it. It may take them six months or even a year to adopt it. You don't have that kind of time. You want to do it, make your mistakes, fail, get going, *now.*

On the other hand, the minister at your second meeting may demur. He may have nothing in writing, or he may have something that isn't suffering service at all. Or he may have done no homework and may not be treating you with the respect you deserve.

Escalate. Get another meeting with him within a week and tell him you will be bringing three of your friends. Make them a good cross-section: male, female, young, old, rich, poor. He may not take *you* seriously, but he must take a movement seriously. That is the point of organization. Every minister is politically astute enough to know when a movement has started in his congregation. And believe me, four people sitting in any minister's office are a movement.

Caution: husbands, don't bring wives; wives, don't bring husbands. Two couples = two families. The minister can handle that. But remember, *you* want to handle *him.* Four individuals = *four* families. Already you have begun to go up geometrically.

The question now becomes at what point does the minister see the suffering servanthood of your actions. If he is still not seeing, then you need another meeting with more people. Then another with more. And another with more until he does see.

But, of course, he may *never* see, and you and your group have to decide whether to go on to Option 2 or Option 3.

*

Option 2. Work around him.

With this option you forget the minister. He is impossible. You do it all on your own.

For my money, this is not an option. How can you run an enterprise without the general manager? If he doesn't agree with what you are doing, he will try to trip you up every step of the way. If he is apathetic, his apathy will kill you. Not immediately but over the long haul. Your strength will be sapped, and even if it isn't *your* strength and *you* could go on forever, it will begin to get to your people. Six months. A year. They will start dropping off. How can you operate, in your spare time, five hours a week, with someone who is paid to do it differently 60–80 hours a week? Correction: 40–60 hours a week. There isn't a minister in the country who works 60–80 hours a week who would not be receptive to at least the possibility of his church's becoming a suffering servant.

*

Option 3. Work without him.

In other words, get rid of him. It is a real option. It is in your power. You are organized.

But there is some question whether you should exercise this option. He may be near retirement. He may be looking for another job anyway. (Better find that out. Ask him.) He may have come to heal a split church and his kind of caretaker regime is just what *is* needed at this time in your church's life. He may have been there only a year and you haven't yet given him a chance to show his stuff. There are a lot of variables. And before you and your group move on this ultimate in escalation, think the variables through. Hard. Better yet: pray them through. Together.

However, it may very well be that the minister should go just the way the baseball manager should go. He isn't getting the best out of the team. He may be lazy. He may be unimaginative. He may be along for the ride. As we have seen, the ministry can easily be a sinecure. The minister has no one watching him. He sets up his own schedule. He reports to no one. It could be the best thing that ever happened to some ministers to be fired.

If you want to fire your minister, at least give him one last chance before you do. Go back to Option I and tell him if he's still not interested, you and your group, after much thought and prayer, have no other option but to ask him to resign. If he refuses, then you escalate, go to the appropriate committees, split the church.

It *may* be the thing to do. Then again it may *not.* You have to *know.* How do you know?

Partial checklist for firing a minister.

1. Does he work a 40-hour week?
2. Has he failed to increase the benevolences?
3. Has he failed to decrease the membership?
4. Has he failed to increase studying?
5. Has he failed to increase sharing?
6. Has he failed to increase serving?
7. Does he belong to the Rotary Club?

*

Option 4. Join another church.

It's a real option. There's no reason why you should stay in your present church if it is not going to move to suffering service. Get with a church that is. It's like hiring a new minister. You have anywhere from 2 to 200 churches in a given city to choose from. Even across traditional boundaries. Plenty of Protestants, for instance, find more suffering service at campus Newman Centers than they do in the Protestant churches in town. Likewise, many Catholics want the freedom of a different style from the one offered by the parish in their neighborhood.

Of course, you have to be honest about whether you are leaving because it is right or because it is convenient. It may be that your job is to organize a church that desperately needs organizing. On the other hand, it may be that, realistically, your church is *so* far from being a suffering servant, with even the minister being against you, that you just don't have the time it would take to organize it. If that were your main job, that would be one thing. But it isn't. Consequently you go to a church that may not be any further along in being a suffering servant, but in which the minister is at least trying.

In the event that you decide to leave, you get an appointment with the minister whose church you are thinking of joining to check out very carefully that you have found the one you want. Ask him the same questions you would if you were hiring him. Make especially certain that he isn't about to leave. It will take you at least three years to get to the point where you can be on the Pastoral Nominating Committees or know who should be.

It's possible, of course, that you don't have friends in this church, so, while you get your minister you lose your group. You have to decide which you want more. You assume, naturally, that you will be able to find new friends in the new church. Or your group could stay together.

You also get an appointment with your present minister to tell him why you are leaving. Then you put it in writing. He'll never forget it. And it might nudge him to future action on behalf of the Suffering Servant.

*

Option 5. Start another church.

The last thing the world needs is a proliferation of sects. But a proliferation of churches may be another matter. And this is perhaps the toughest decision you have to make: whether or not to start up your own church and run it from scratch as a suffering servant. You would do so, presumably, only if none of the other churches in town was being run that way and would not be run that way, as far as you can see, in the near future.

Now there is nothing new or suspect about house churches. That's what all the churches were in the 1st century and it may be what all the churches will end up being in the 20th. The reason is power. A good house church is equivalent to a normal "church" 20 times its size.

Say there 20 families in a house church. Say the average income is $15,000. Naturally all the families tithe. That's a budget of $30,000. Generally a "church" has to have at least 300–400 "members" before it can muster a budget that size.

But there are drawbacks. One is that it will take time and you will have to be *the* leader. You may not be prepared for either. Another is that you may be cutting yourself out of a lot of potential. There may be no real reason you and your friends couldn't stay in your church and use all that money and enthusiasm to inspire others in the church. You have a built-in constituency. Outside, your constituency may be harder to come by.

However, there is more to it than that. You will obviously have only a part-time nonpaid general manager. Namely you. That may be fine for a while. But a year or two out to sea and you may be hurting. For one thing, even as a part-time job it isn't your thing. You're an accountant, not a part-time minister, and you just may not be the man/woman for the job. For another thing, two years out to sea and you're going to be, very possibly, in the same bureaucratic fix most fledgling organizations are. You're big, say, you're booming. Who's going to staff it? Where are you going to house it? Inevitably you, or some of your people, are going to begin thinking those thoughts. And then the first thing that will happen is that your 1:1 giving will slip. People will start talking mortgage. You will be in great danger of losing all your standards of suffering service because you "need members" to "pay off the mortgage." And so on. In a word, you run the serious risk of becoming just another "church."

Consequently, it might be worthwhile to consider *being* a house church but *staying* in your present church. That way you get all the advantages of a bureaucracy that has made its mistakes (as you and your friends are only too happy to point out). And you have the advantage of an institution that will no doubt be around long after you and/or your friends move away, lose enthusiasm, die off.

However, having said that, if the minister won't budge, and if you don't want to or can't get him fired, and if in your considered and prayerful judgment the congregation will not move around him, and if there is no other local church interested in servanthood, then you should consider Option 5. Even if you fold or go bureaucratic in two years, you have had the most spiritual experience of your life. The Spirit is released in small groups as nowhere else. Maybe it's because you have no professional to lean on—no minister to do *your* preaching, no director of Christian education to do *your* teaching, no choir director to do *your* music, no youth director to relate to *your* kids. If Option 5 increases *your* suffering service *and* the suffering service of the largest possible number of people, then Option 5 is for you.

TEN

How to Keep
Your Minister Organized

I

One of the biggest problems in churches is the ministerial copout. "I wanted to do it but my laymen (they always say "men") wouldn't go along with me." That's baloney. The point of leadership is to lead. If they didn't go along with him it's because he didn't get them to go along with him. He was not bright.

The problem is serious, deep-rooted, pandemic. It is the old question: Who runs the church? In an access of revolt against Roman Catholic hierarchism, virtually all Protestant denominations stripped the clergyman of any power to *run* the church. All the minister has the power to do is preach the sermon and administer the sacraments. But since any church member who can read is perfectly capable of doing those things, the minister has virtually no power at all.

This is, however, an absurd misreading of how any enterprise is run. You have to have *someone* responsible for seeing that it is run. In a church this is the minister. It is also of course, the official board of the church. But a board is a board. And while it may and certainly should set policy, it does not execute policy. That is the job of the chief executive officer. That is what he is *hired* to *do*.

Consequently it is self-serving for any minister to say he/she

96

wanted to do it, but lay/they didn't. Often, perhaps most often, the board wants it done, and they are "they." The problem was that he/she didn't get it done.

*

The ministerial copout takes another form. "It's not my job. They hired me to preach and teach. That's what I was trained for." Baloney again. If that's all you were trained for then you should be an evangelist or a teacher. The fact was you chose the ministry. And the facts of that decision dictate that you wanted to plan, you wanted to execute, you wanted to lead. Either stick by your decision or quit.

Still, the problem persists and is subtle. Ministers honestly feel ill-equipped to administrate a $50,000, 500-member enterprise, let alone a $1/4-of-a-million one with 2,500 members. If this is the case, they should be trained. Either they should not be hired without that seminary course in planning, or, if they are hired, the church, as we have seen, should pay for such a course *now* and for a retread every three years.

Even this, of course, may not assuage a minister's honest feeling of inferiority to many of his men who are running large enterprises of their own. It is this feeling that breeds the "I-had-a-great-idea-but-they-wouldn't-execute-it" syndrome. He feels they are more *equipped* to execute it, and if they don't, that's the end of it.

But that most emphatically is not the end of it. The minister doesn't propose and the congregation dispose. He is the full-time, paid professional, and in most churches he is the *only* full-time paid professional. He is paid to execute the plan. If something doesn't get done it is his fault. That doesn't mean he does everything. That would be impossible. But it does mean that he is *responsible* for seeing that everything gets done. That's what he is paid for.

Furthermore, the minister has no business feeling inferior to his men. He is in command of the greatest enterprise in the world. That is job enough for anyone.

*

A third ministerial copout is to leave. Statistics are hard to come by, but the average Protestant tenure is probably only 3–5 years. They wouldn't buy my plan, the minister says in effect. Therefore I will go on to another town.

In the first place, the "town" is invariably a city and the salary fat. You never hear of a minister "accepting a call" to a smaller church. That renders his exit suspect.

In the second place, it is all too often not a matter of the congregations' not buying the minister's plan but of the minister's not offering them any plan to buy. As we have seen, a plan by its very nature is going to take 1–2 years to write. Then it is going to take 1–2 years even to begin to implement it. Therefore anyone playing musical chairs after only 3–5 years cannot be taken seriously as a minister. He is a dilettante.

In the third place, however, there *are* exceptions. It is possible that a minister should leave after 3–5 years. It is even possible that he should have left before that. Early divorces are often better than late.

How do you know if you have a square peg in a round hole? Some indications are:

1. If the preaching drops off.
2. If the hours put in on the job drop off. (Since nobody ever knows what hours a minister works, this information is not easy to come by.)
3. If the worship services are dull.
4. If he makes little or no contribution in committee meetings.
5. If there are no new ideas for church "program."
6. If he wants to build a building.
7. If he takes no interest in the Nominating Committee.
8. If he refuses, as a matter of principle, to know what everyone gives.
9. If he doesn't know the name of the local leader of his political party.
10. If he joins the Rotary Club.

Obviously the best way to guard against this type of thing is to take your time in selecting your new minister. There are more ministers than churches, so you have no reason not to take your time. Long courtships are often wise. Slowly and carefully, all the subjects noted so far should be discussed. Then if he's not your man, no matter how much pressure you are getting from the congregation ("attendance is falling off," "the offering is down"), go for another.

II

Obviously the minister needs a support group for his planning. He gets it in four places:

One, from his own church. In any church in America 3% of the people are ready to go. Within three months any minister worth his salt will know who they are. No matter how large the congregation, they will have surfaced. If they haven't surfaced, then they are not among the 3%. Now this is not to say others will not surface along the way. Obviously they will. Nor is it to say that those who surface first will necessarily last. They may leave town, die, run out of gas. It is only to say that, *at any given time,* the 3% *are* there and they *will* support the minister in his planning. In a congregation of 300, this means nine. In a congregation of 1,000, 30.

*

Two, the minister gets support from one, maybe two colleagues.

In any given association or presbytery or diocese there will always be at least one other minister and sometimes two who will immediately buy the style of the church as suffering servant. Their encouragement, advice, and counsel are invaluable. More to the point, their sharing of their failures in pulling off the style is crucial.

Note that I have stayed with the denomination. That is not to say that ministers in other denominations do not have a lot to offer. Obviously they have, as we shall see below. It is only to say that the problems peculiar to one denomination are peculiar to that denomination. A minister needs as much inside help as he can get.

*

Three, the minister gets support from around the country. The Christian church is a big enterprise. And big things are going on everywhere. He can hear about them through such organizations as the Academy of Parish Clergy, 3100 West Lake Street, Minneapolis, Minnesota 55416.

Better yet, it is time for the serious ministers to unionize, to form their own "church." There is too much risk alone. Congregations are zapping the really creative ministers right and left. But if 14 *other* churches in town are struck on Sunday morning, that is a different matter.

I say 14 because this is how many other really top-flight ministers there will be in any major metropolitan area. There will be at least two Catholics, and at least two each of the major denominations: Baptist, Methodist, Presbyterian, Episcopal, United Church of Christ. There will also be at least two from the smaller, more conservative churches. And there will often be one Jew. (Remember, the Suffering Servant began with Isaiah.)

It could be called the American Clergy Association. (You can't use "minister" or "pastor" because of Catholics and Jews.) It would *not* be for everyone. It would be only for those men and women who were committed to making their churches into suffering servants. That means they would have to be committed, as a matter of principle and from the beginning, to:

1. Trim their membership by 1/3 within the next two years.
2. Build nothing that is not matched, dollar for dollar, with benevolences.
3. Submit a plan to others in the local union, annually, for approval.
4. See that the plan came from the congregation as well as themselves and be held accountable by the other local union members for the process whereby that was done.
5. See that the plan is based on the image of Jesus as the

Suffering Servant, and see that the plan is based on the sermons in which that is done.

6. See that the plan contains certain minimal standards of membership.
7. See that those standards reflect the first church's *kerygma, koinonia, diakonia.*
8. Set up a 5-year plan to match every dollar their church spends on itself with a dollar to benevolences.
9. Include matching their mortgage for benevolences.
10. Lose their union membership if they fail in the 5-year plan.
11. Lose their union membership if they fail to submit an annual plan.
12. Lose their union membership if they fail to support each other in a strike.
13. Lose their union membership if they fail to make a quarterly meeting except in case of serious illness or emergency.
14. Lose their union membership if they fail to pay annual dues of 1% of their salaries.

The union is necessary for the following reasons: *(a)* As a support group for the ministers who are trying to lead their churches into suffering service.

(b) As a means of putting the heat on denominations to accept their responsibility—namely, getting all the churches within their jurisdiction to become suffering servants, too. The best way to convince anyone of anything is to show him it works. The local union members would go to their respective denominations and say: "Look, we've been into this for a year, two years, three years. It works. Here are the results. Now you go after the other churches in the denomination. You match our heat. You can even go slower on the money" (p.131).

(c) As a way of crossing denominational lines. If the Consultation on Church Union (COCU; see Appendix 3) is ever going to work, if any structural ecumenicity is going to work, people have to *see* it working. A tight local union of 15 people would show the ecumeni-

cally minded that people can work together structurally, that what happens at your church dramatically affects what happens at my church. You demonstrate, in living color, that the ridiculous atomism that has always afflicted American church life is at last on its way out. That people can do things together, and that when the going gets tough they can still do things together.

(d) As a demonstration to the country and even the world that the church means business. That it is a force to be reckoned with in American life. That it is more than the grinning hyenas on the Saturday church advertisement page (at reduced rates).

It is one thing for a clergyman here, a clergyman there, quietly to get lynched. It is quite another thing for 15 local clergy, Protestant *and* Catholic *and* Jewish, to hang together if any one hangs separately. If he goes, they go. That is impact. That is power. *That* is organization.

(e) As a means of upgrading the profession. The clergy are not more notably qualified for their jobs than others with graduate degreees are for theirs. A professional union, with only the highest standards, would not only attract the best people in the profession. It would attract the best people *to* the profession. It would also raise the level of the entire profession because members would at last have something to shoot for. They would *know* what professional standards of performance were. They could *measure* their growth.

*

Four, the minister gets support from the Holy Spirit.

That may sound mystical. Fine. It's the same mysticism that enabled the first church to do in the first century what we are trying to do in the 20th. Indeed, if it is not done, many are predicting the church, as we know it, will not make it out of the century. It will be in exile.

Everybody—Joan of Arc, Savonarola, Dietrich Bonhoeffer, John Bunyan, the Apostle Paul, Martin Luther King, Jeremiah, Pope John —everybody who ever tried to do what the Suffering Servant did found that he had the support he needed all along. No, it wasn't natural. It wasn't inevitable. It wasn't easy to feel the support. "My God, my God, why hast thou forsaken me?" Jesus himself cried (Matt. 27:46). But the support *was* there.

I can do all things in him who strengthens me (Phil. 4:13).

All things are possible with God (Mark 10:27).

He who endures to the end will be saved (Matt. 10:22).

It is not you who speak, but the Spirit of your Father speaking through you (Matt. 10:20).

It is not *you* who are doing these things. You could not do them. You could not be a suffering servant. They are beyond you. They are *impossible.* That is the *point.* God *is* what you find yourself doing as a suffering servant that *you* could never have done.

III

Nevertheless, having said all this, there are still some objections to the minister as planner.

Here's how the three most common run:

One stock objection to asking the minister to plan is that he will do it all and the Holy Spirit will not do it *at* all.

But that is not true. The Spirit is doing it all the time. The minister reads. The minister prays. The minister listens. He, of all people, wants the plan to be written, revised, checked, edited *through* him, not *by* him. He is trained to be used. He is trained to wait. He is trained to be passive. "Of this gospel I *was made* a minister" (Eph. 3:7).

Nobody *wants* to be a minister. Who would want to lead people into a different lifestyle? Who would want to go against the grain of his culture? Who would want to risk rejection, job loss, emotional upset? The minister, of all people, has already experienced the Holy Spirit. If he hadn't, he wouldn't be where he was. He "was made" a minister. He didn't volunteer.

Now this is no guarantee, of course, that the minister will continue to be used by the Spirit. But any congregation concerned about his continued "use" should remember that the ministry, of all professions, operates under one classic and tough restraint—the Bible. The minister can plan until he's blue in the face, but if that plan doesn't square with the Bible, it's out. And the minister knows it's out.

That's why the sermon is so important. It keeps the minister in *weekly* touch with the Bible. If a minister preaches poorly, watch out. It's the first sign that his planning is going awry. If a minister won't do the homework in the Bible necessary for good preaching, then he's using the Spirit rather than being used by it. He is not putting *his* planning in line with *God's* planning. He has eliminated the classic and tough restraint. Remember:

> If this plan . . . is of men, it will fail; but if it is of God, you will not be able to overthrow them (Acts 5:38–39).

*

Another objection to the minister as planner goes like this. We're hiring a pastor, not a robot. We want a human being, not a computer. We want a planner who is a person, not a planning machine.

Of course. Couldn't agree more. I am simply emphasizing the one thing "pulpit committees" do *not* emphasize. They will ask all the usual questions. Can he preach? Can he teach? Can he counsel? Can he get along with teenagers? Can he lead in community affairs? Can he evangelize? Can he visit the sick? Can he moderate a meeting? And so on.

All very good questions. All questions that must be asked. But all questions that will be asked. The question that is not asked is: Can you *plan?*

Second, the objection implies an implicit disparagement of planning which is illicit. It says, in effect, you get a person who is a hot-shot planner and he will be a cold human being. He may be able to write a plan but he won't be able to relate to people.

Not at all. For one thing, it disparages every human being who makes his or her living planning. It disparages the executive. It disparages the labor leader. It disparages the politician. It disparages the mother, who plans the meals, plans the recreation, plans the bedtime stories.

For another thing, it disparages Christ. He had a plan. He would preach the word. He would heal the sick. He would go to Jerusalem. He would let himself be killed. But that plan, about which he was relentless and from which no one could dissuade him—not even his closest friend (Matt. 16:22–23)—that plan did not interfere with his relationships to people. Indeed, it enhanced them. It took him to people he would never have met otherwise. It allowed him to have time for them. It allowed him to inspire them. It allowed him to be human with them.

Third, it is precisely the planner who is *more* concerned with people than the average person. He knows that the only way for his plan to work is for people to work it. That means they have to be consulted. It means he has to know what moves them to act. It means he has to be sensitive to their wants, needs, frustrations. The politician is *closer* to people. That's how he gets elected. He knows what they want. The executive is *closer* to people. That's how he gets promoted. He knows how to get the best from his employees. He knows how to give them *his* best.

Fourth, O.K. So Hitler was a good planner. He knew how to fit a whole nation into his plan.

The argument is reductionist and therefore suspect. But it does have an element of validity. The minister *uses* people to fit his plan.

On the one hand, yes, precisely. That is the point of his being called as the minister. But *(a)* it is not his plan, it is theirs together, and *(b)* it is not theirs alone, it is God's. That sounds arrogant, but consider. It comes from the Bible. It is continually checked and balanced by the church. It is never disagreed with in its fundamentals. No one can argue, Biblically, with the Suffering Servant, the *kerygma,* the *koinonia,* the *diakonia.* They are all there. They *were* the first church.

Therefore the point of the church, its *raison d'être, is* to "use" people. It is to "get" them all, including the minister, to "fit into the plan." The church's job is to "make disciples of all nations" (Matt. 28:19). And the minister's job is to keep "his" church producing toward that end.

Furthermore, we all "use" people all the time. It is part of the human condition. It is a fact of life. It is sin. God *uses* a sinful minister to prod a sinful people. In the same way a husband "uses" his wife and a wife "uses" her husband. We "use" the other to fill our need to be loved. The President "uses" the nation to fill its need for direction which in turn fills his need to lead.

*

Third objection. All this is too "goal-oriented" for me. I want my religion to happen. I don't want it to be planned.

Fine if it happens that way. But does it? Did it? As we have seen, you very likely got your religion because somebody planned it. You were converted at a rally? Somebody planned the rally. You were converted in confirmation? Somebody planned the church which planned the confirmation. You were converted at home? Somebody, namely your parents, planned it that way.

But even if that is not the way it happened, you still, as we have seen, can't escape planning. Paul is always cited as the "unplanned" Christian, the one for whom Christ "happened." But the facts were *(a)* that Paul was *already* operating on a plan, albeit a wrong one, to persecute Christians; *(b)* another person, Ananias, included him in *his* plan (Acts 9:10*b*); *(c)* Paul was so dumfounded by what happened to him that he said *it* was planned.

> Christ died for our sins in *accordance with the scriptures*. . . . Then . . . he appeared to me. . . . By the *grace of God* I am what I am (1 Cor. 15:3, 7, 8, 10).

We may not like to plan, but we *are planned.* It is "a *plan* for the fullness of time, to unite all things in him" (Eph. 1:10). That is the Good News. That is the miracle. That is what the church celebrates. That is the plan of God every minister wants to get his people in line with. And to do that he has to plan how he and they are going to do it. He has to allow himself to *be* planned, *be* programmed, to *do* the Ananias thing for every potential Paul in and beyond his congregation. Otherwise it may happen, to be sure. But then again it may not. More to the point, it has not. The number of Christians in the world is on the decrease. And, since that may be just what we need, the power of the Christians left is *not* on the increase. Look at Vietnam. Look at Biafra. Look at the nuclear weapon equivalent of 15 tons of TNT for every man, woman, and child on the face of the planet.

It is time for the church to do what it was called to do.

> To me . . . this grace was given . . . to make all men see what is the *plan* of the mystery hidden for all ages in God. . . ; that through the *church* the manifold wisdom of God might now be made known (Eph. 3:8–10).

*

Fourth objection. Isn't this just catering to the clergy martyr complex?

How so? Who ever said the clergy have a martyr complex? They are no different from anyone else. They have no more desire to be crucified than the next person. What *they* do that others don't, however, is that they are *hired* to remind churches that Christ said:

> If any man would come after me, let him deny himself and take up his cross and follow me (Matt. 16:24).

That is their *job*. It has nothing to do with a martyr complex. It has everything to do with doing what they were hired to do. The marvel is not that clergymen *are* crucified by churches. But that they aren't. In other words, the clergy aren't doing their jobs. Which means that they and their congregations never reminded each other what that job was when they were hired. Blame both.

*

Fifth objection. All right, take the other tack. Doesn't this make the clergyman a superman? To measure up to this kind of job description, he will have to be Joan of Arc, Sir Thomas More, and the Apostle Paul rolled into one.

Not at all. Again the argument is reductionist and therefore suspect. He is doing no more nor less than reminding people what Jesus told them to do. He is paid, in other words, to read them the Bible. Therefore if you call him superman you have to call all Christians supermen. Jesus gave us all impossible jobs. Remember: Go the second mile, turn the other cheek, love your enemy are impossible. "With men it is impossible" (Mark 10:27). That was the point. To be told to do something you couldn't do. Of course it was superhuman. That was the point. To give you something beyond ("super") your ability so you would be *thrown* onto God. God *is* what we do when *we* cannot do it.

> By grace you have been saved through faith; and this is *not* your own doing, it is the gift of God—not because of works, lest any man should boast. For we are his workmanship (Eph. 2:8).

*

Sixth objection. All right, so how do you handle failure? You set up your plan. You get everybody shaped up or shipped out. You can't miss.

Precisely wrong. You're missing all the time. That is the point of the plan. To show you how you fail, not how you succeed. It is a humbling experience. Why? Because you don't study enough. You don't share enough. You don't serve enough. You are anything *but* a suffering servant. The closer you come the farther you realize you are. You are "the least of the apostles" (1 Cor. 15:9).

The point of the work is that the work doesn't work. That is precisely the point you are trying to make with your plan. The problem with churches is that they limit themselves to "can do" projects. But a plan won't let them get away with it. The plan shows them they can't do what they are required to do. Therefore they have to be thrown onto God.

We study, share, serve. *Then* we are saved. No, you don't *have* to study, share, serve to be saved. "The wind blows where it wills" (John 3:8). There are *no* conditions of grace. No plans. Repeat: no plans. But, it may be that you, middle-class American Christian, mesmerized by your ability to think, feel, and act, do have to have it proved to you, by your church, that you *can't* think, feel, act enough. And that the only way you can be saved is not by saving yourself. That has to be proved to you. You have to *be* saved. You *can't* study. You *can't* share. You *can't* serve. Therefore it has to be God because it couldn't be you. When you read a book you couldn't care less about, that *is* God. When you give away 10% of your hard-earned cash, that *is* God. When you put yourself aside for someone else, that *is* God. When you find yourself at a lousy political meeting at 1:00 in the morning for 30 units of low-income housing in your suburb, that *is* God. Why? Because it couldn't be you. You wouldn't do it. "This is not *your* own doing" (Eph. 2:8). The church are the people who *can't* do it. Who fail. It is when they fail that they begin to succeed. We have all these "successful" churches all over America. That's the trouble. They haven't failed. A plan gets them to fail. It crucifies them.

ELEVEN

How to Introduce the Plan to Your Church

The plan is introduced to the congregation in the following ways:

First, it is preached, part by part, while the parts are being written. The minister gives the congregation the Biblical background for each part of the plan before the plan is "sprung" on the people. This way the plan will not be sprung. It will evolve. It will be as natural, 4–24 months later, as leaves to a tree. We handed the plan to every church member after a service. There was hardly a question. It was assumed this was the direction the church was going because for months they had been in dialogue about it.

*

Second, it is shared, part by part, while the parts are being written, with the congregation for their input on each part. This means that the congregation, in as many small groups as possible, studies the Book of Acts, shares their feelings about the Book of Acts and about each other, serves the community. It does not mean that the congregation studies the official board's plan. It studies the Book of Acts from which the plan will come and to which plan they can make a hefty contribution by the way they have studied, shared, and served the Book of Acts.

110

This way the focus is kept clear. The focus is not on the plan (which has not yet been written). It is not on this book. *It is on the first Christians and what they did to "turn the world upside down" (Acts 17:6).* That's where the action is. There are too many "programs" making the rounds of too many churches. That is not the point at all. The point is the Holy Spirit and how the congregation is being led to plan.

*

Third, the plan is written by the minister. As we have seen, it can't be written by anyone else. He is the chief executive officer and he writes the plan. If he doesn't want to write the plan, then he need not be your minister.

Upon reflection, it is obvious that he is the one to write. *(a)* He has already done the homework in the Bible. That is what he was hired to do. *(b)* He has already spoken about it in his sermons. That is what he was hired to do. *(c)* He is the one who stands most to lose from the success or failure of the institution. Therefore he is most motivated to write the plan. That is what he was hired to do. *(d)* He is the one closest to the most action, day in and day out. In other words, he is the best equipped to write the plan. That is what he was hired to do.

However, this does not mean that the plan is solely the minister's plan. What he writes *has already been said by the congregation* to each other in the small groups. It has also already been said by him in the sermons. Thus they plan together. It is neither their plan nor his. It has come out of their "Life Together," as Bonhoeffer put it. It is not handed down from on high. It is organic to the greatest extent it can be.

Having said that, however, the minister cannot abdicate. This is a 51%-49% partnership: 51% minister, 49% congregation. As we saw earlier (see p. 10), the minister gets the extra percent because he is the one who is hired to present the Suffering Servant, hired to get the plan written, hired to get it executed. That is his job. The buck stops with him. He is responsible. A dead church always means a dead minister.

*

Fourth, the plan is approved by the official board. Not by parliamentary procedure but by consensus. If it isn't obvious that this should be the plan, then you have to go back to the process. Perhaps a simple rewrite is enough. Perhaps it needs more small grouping or more reading.

Or, it may need the elimination of certain members of the official board. Fortunately there is a limit to length of board membership in any congregation. Usually it is three years. That means that three years after the minister arrives he should have the board he wants. Make it four years at the most. If he doesn't, he isn't organized. You can bet your life every chairman of every board of directors of every company in America has *just* the people on his board with whom he feels he can work. If he doesn't, then it is doubtful he has what it takes to remain chairman. The president has his cabinet and the minister has his official board. He does *whatever is necessary* in the nominating process to see that he gets the people he wants.

There is no reason to be uptight about the amount of time it may take to get the plan officially signed, sealed, and delivered. For one thing, the church has always moved glacially on everything. So you do not exacerbate sensibilities by moving slowly. More important, taking your time can only help the process. More people get exposed to the planning. More people read the Bible. More people get the message on Sunday morning. And so on.

*

Fifth, the plan is printed. Not mimeographed. Printed. This is *it* for your congregation. You want it in cement. You don't want the usual two-bit church mimeograph job. You mean business. And you want everyone in the congregation to know it. And you want everyone considering being in the congregation to know it.

Now this does not mean you cannot revise the plan. Obviously you can and should, regularly. Planning is never finished. The minister's job is to keep planning. So is the congregation's.

What it does mean is that this is the basic document for your congregation for this year. It is how you spell out the Book of Acts. It is how you spell out Jesus' plan of suffering service.

Then you issue two annual supplements, one fall, one spring. They present, in more detail, the study programs offered, the share programs offered, the serve programs offered: fall and winter, spring and summer. These are mimeographed (if you have a good machine) or printed, using lots of space, illustrations, etc.

Incidentally, the printing costs will not be that much, since the plan will be short and to the point. It need not even be as long as the one in Chapter 3.

*

Sixth, the plan is mailed with the weekly or biweekly or monthly newsletter. This way you can be sure everyone gets it. The annual report is mailed to stockholders. Surely the annual plan can be mailed to church members.

*

Seventh, the deacons, the accountability committee (of which more later), the official board, the minister, call on all members within a month of the issuance of the plan.

The point is obviously to answer any questions, elicit ideas, interpret, cajole, inspire. In larger churches the month may have to be extended to two or even three months. At any rate, *every member must be called on.*

The call has its own dynamic. For one thing, the person called on will be so amazed the church is calling on him for something other than money that he will be immediately receptive. For another thing, you are there not only to interpret but to elicit. People are flattered to think their ideas are sought. And they are sought. It isn't flattery. Again, no one has a corner on creativity, and a 14-year-old member who hasn't been in church since the day she joined may have a terrific idea for one of the three areas next time around. So may an 80-year-old.

This is a step, incidentally, which we at our church did not take. The entire planning process would have benefited if we had.

*

Eighth, the plan is sent to the denominational judicatories—local, state, national.

It may, of course, be an exercise in futility. But if enough churches start sending in their plans the higher judicatories just may accept their responsibility. That responsibility is simply and precisely to keep the local churches planning. It is to keep their feet to the fire. If that sounds harsh, it is. One reason we are in the mess we are in the Protestant church is that *no* higher judicatory in America dares to stick it to the local church. There is nothing about dues, nothing about assessments, nothing about the *taxes* you *owe* to feed starving people. There are *no* standards for membership whatever. Every church is allowed to go its merry way and there are *no* sanctions if it doesn't produce.

Shipping off your church's plan tells the higher judicatory that you favor this kind of accountability. If other churches do the same, the higher judicatory will get the message. It wants the message. It has wanted to flex its muscle all along. But it has not seen support at the grass roots. This way you get the message through loud and clear that there is support (see Appendix 2).

TWELVE

How to Sell the Plan
to Your Church

I

One key to the execution of the plan is new members. In spite of the fact that total church membership is declining, people are still joining churches. The key is to get them to join on the right terms. As we have seen, virtually everyone joins the church without realizing that certain things are expected of them when they join the organization of the Suffering Servant.

There are certain things that must be done with any potential member.

First, the old "membership class" routine is out. Not that it was a poor idea but that it was poorly executed. For a half hour before or after church the minister would discuss "the beliefs of the church," "the structure of the church," "the polity of the church." No good: *(a)* no room for dialogue; *(b)* no room for what matters most—namely, what Joe Doakes is going to do in the form of suffering service because he has joined the church.

Second, there is no use wasting time on "the beliefs of the church" in the 1970s. That is not where it's at any more. You aren't a Christian because of what you believe but because of what you do. It's silly to waste time on the Virgin Birth when you should be spending your

115

time on the atrocious infant mortality rate in Blue Cross (yes, cross) hospitals. "Christians" have risen on Sunday mornings to shout, sing, dance, murmur, applaud what they believe, but then they have dropped napalm on yellow babies on Monday. It doesn't make sense. More to the point: it isn't the Suffering Servant.

Third, the minister calls on the potential member. You can have all the other people in the world calling, but at one time, before a person joins, the minister calls. After all, he is the chief executive officer and he is "hiring" a top-management employee. The employee has a job to do and if he doesn't like the job description he need not join the "firm."

The minister lays out the Study-Share-Serve plan and both shows and elicits how the potential member buys in or doesn't. If he doesn't, then he doesn't join. If he does, he signs. There is a contract. "If you . . . keep my covenant, you shall be my . . . possession" (Exod. 19:5). The contract is simply his/her name, address, telephone on the detachable last page of, respectively, the Study, Share, and Serve brochures.

Fourth, the new member is immediately "assimilated" as he/she fulfills his/her three commitments. But let's be frank. He will not fill all three with equal enthusiasm. He may be at that point in his life where he needs social action but does not need theological reflection. Conversely, he may be at the point where he needs theological reflection but does not need social action. As a Christian, however, he needs *all three.* And it is the job of the minister to see that the appropriate people—it may be the deacons, it may be a committee, it may be the minister himself—stimulate (and irritate) the member to *do* all three. Peter was ready for sharing with Jesus. He was not ready for social action with Jesus. He was not ready to go to Jerusalem. Jesus called him "Satan" to his face (Matt. 16:23). Peter went.

II

The gut problem, however, is how to sell the plan to old members. New members are no problem. They buy the plan or they don't join.

But the old members are something else. They joined on different terms. The wrong ones, namely, no terms. They simply stood up, pledged allegiance to Jesus, and that was that. Nothing about standards of suffering service. Nothing about requirements. Nothing about commands. Nothing about obedience. "A new *commandment* I give you," Jesus said (John 13:34).

First, face up to the fact that you are going to lose members. It is the only way to operate effectively in the 1970s. In our case we lost one-third. That is to say, of the 270 people who were members of the church during the first six months I was there, 96, over the course of the next several years, dropped out. As one man put it in the offering plate: "This pays up our pledge. We're leaving the church because we don't like the new minister." Fine.

Second, there should not be an ounce of guilt over the membership loss. No church should be so imperialistic as to think it has the only way to salvation. If people's spiritual needs can be met better elsewhere, let them go. They should go. The only thing that counts is that they go somewhere where they *will* become suffering servants. If all they do in your church is suffer, then they should find a place where they can serve as well.

Third, face up to the fact that people will continue to leave. Even the people who buy in to the plan before they join will leave. We lose about 5% a year this way. They don't like the standards. They don't like the social action. They don't like our giving to starving people at the expense of giving to the parking lot.

> Please cancel my pledge. . . . For years I thought my anti-Christian feelings stemmed from attending churches which were not truly Christian. I thought that if I found a church which really tried to relate our present-day world to the teachings of Christ, all would be well. I believe St. Luke is such a church.
>
> I deeply admire St. Luke's efforts, but I don't believe I am a Christian by anyone's definition. Nor do I believe in living "for others." It *is* crazy, and to me that is very rarely the point. Only rarely am I in the mood to do crazy things. My doing for others is limited to "when the

cost is small." . . . I believe yours is a wonderful, crazy congregation.
(And) I hope you will grant me the privilege of visiting you when I am
in one of my crazy moods.

Fourth, membership loss should always be kept in perspective. We
lost 96 but we gained 500. You lose 33% but you gain 200%. We
dropped 10% in pledging units last year but income was up. In 1971
there were 159 pledging units and total income was $126,472. In 1972
there were 142 pledging units and total income was $128,153.

Fifth, having said all this, however, a church does everything it can
to keep a member before the member decides to go. This means at
least the following:

(a) A deacon makes a call at the first sign of slippage. The signs
are obvious: lack of church attendance for over a month, lack of
pledge payments, lack of performance in any of the three areas, vibra-
tions from other members, etc. The deacon calls. The person airs the
problem. The deacon suggests he contact the person with whom he
has the problem (it is nearly always personal in churches). The deacon
says he will also contact the person. They work together on a creative
solution. The disaffected member does not just ventilate.

The deacon also challenges the disaffected member with the gamut
of study-share-serve possibilities. He knows the person well enough
from previous calls to know where he needs to grow and how best to
work with him and his commitments. The deacon doesn't back off.
He knows this is one of the important assignments of his life. It is
serious business.

By the same token, the deacon is there to learn. No one has a corner
on creativity and the member may well have some excellent suggestions for improving the three areas. The deacon accepts challenges as
well as gives them.

(b) If the slippage continues for three months, the deacon calls
again. Same type of call.

(c) If the slippage continues, a member of the official board calls.
Same type of call.

(d) If the slippage continues for three more months, the minister calls. Same type of call.

(e) If the slippage continues, the member is dropped from the rolls. You can't spend all your time coddling disaffected members. The doctor doesn't coddle disaffected patients. If they don't like his style, they go to another doctor. He does not pursue them. He has his hands full with the people who do like his style. It is the same with a company and its employees and its customers. It was the same with Jesus.

> If any one will not receive you or listen to your words, shake off the dust from your feet as you leave that house or town (Matt. 10:14).

THIRTEEN

How to Organize the Money

The money is where it's at in any institution. Not the only place, of course, but an important place. The church is no exception. The church budget is a precise indicator of what that church feels is important. Virtually every church budget in America shows that the church feels it is more important to give to itself than to give itself in suffering service to others. According to the latest statistics, churches spend 4 times (sic) on themselves what they do on others. 80% to the church, 20% to benevolences.

Part of your plan, the most important part, is to get your church budget to reflect the values of the Suffering Servant. Why the *most* important? Because all the rhetoric in the world is no good if it is not backed up with action. And the action, like it or not, for most Americans, is where the money is. Our money is where our values are. The family checkbook is a precise indicator of what that family values. So is the church's checkbook. So is the corporation's. So is the government's.

One, call the stewardship chairman. Tell him you want to have lunch with him. (That's neutral ground—not the church, not his house, not your house.) And that you want to discuss the budget—specifically next year's budget. (This year's is already a lost cause.)

Two, at the meeting tell him you and your seven friends want to see the budget reflect the values of the church. That means one dollar for benevolences for every dollar of operating—excluding debt retirement, at least this time around (see p. 131). Tell him that you and your friends have done a little homework and that if the operating expenses are kept about where they are and the benevolence giving is increased by $x\%$ a year for the next 5 years you will make it. Then tell him you and your friends are willing to increase your own giving by 1% of your incomes each year for the next 5 until you are tithing (or beyond the tithe). Or that you will tithe beginning now.

He may, of course, demur. He will applaud your own giving but will deplore the congregation's. He will say your goal is impossible because "people will never give that much." He will then tell you what the average gift is and compute what the increase would be "per pledging unit."

Then it will be your turn to demur. You will do it on the basis of the Bible, the tithe, the Suffering Servant, the Holy Spirit. You will remind him that "all things are possible with God" (Mark 10:27). And you will tell him that you and your friends are willing to help sell the idea to the congregation. When could he meet with you to work out the plan?

Three, if he still demurs, escalate. Go to the minister. Do the same thing with him that you did with the stewardship chairman. In many cases this will be enough to deliver the chairman. The minister isn't dumb. He knows where his salary is coming from. He also knows a good first-class revolt when he sees one. It is entirely possible he can get to the stewardship chairman where you can't.

Four, if the minister also demurs, escalate. Ask him when the next meeting of the budget committee is. Take your seven friends. You will outnumber the committee 2–1. Budget decisions are always made by a few—at least at first, before they reach the official board. This will show you mean business. Lean on the committee hard. Tell them it must be done. That it's the only way you can read the Bible. That you're willing to increase your own giving dramatically. That you're willing also to do anything to help.

Five, if the committee demurs, escalate again. Tell the chairman of the official board that you and some of your friends want time on the next agenda to talk about next year's budget. Take twice as many of your friends as there are members of the official board. If you can't muster that many, then you aren't organized. Wait until you can.

At the meeting come on loud and clear. Tell about your three prior fruitless meetings. Tell about your Bible reading. Tell about your prayer with your friends. Tell about the Suffering Servant. Tell about your willingness to give and to help. Some of the board are bound to be with you. If it is obvious you don't have a large majority, don't push. (You have already pushed more than they have ever been pushed before. No one has ever done this to them. It has its own dynamic.) Tell them you'd be happy for them to defer it till the next meeting, pray about it, talk with you and your friends about it between meetings, etc.

Between the meetings assign two or more of your friends to one each of the official board. Take them out to lunch. Answer any questions. Communicate your enthusiasm. Tell them you have $x thousand pledged *already* just from your group.

Six, at the next meeting of the official board go for a decision. If it is positive (with a strong majority), you are on your way. If it isn't, you have a choice: come at them again or designate your money. You *tell* them you have this choice, and you *ask* them which they recommend. By now you will represent anywhere from $10,000 to $20,000 or more, so they will not be interested in letting you designate.

Seven, if, at a third meeting of the board, they still won't go for your position—or for a reasonable facsimile which you have negotiated with them and can live with—escalate to the nominating committee. Do with them exactly as you have done with the stewardship committee to make certain that *your* people are up for office next time. Normally a third of the board will be leaving each year. Within two years, then, you can have two-thirds of the board. Three years, all of it.

Eight, consider prayerfully with your group whether this is the church for you. It could be argued that if you have to push this hard on such a fundamental issue, which should be as noncontroversial as the Lord's Prayer, you should "shake off the dust from your feet" (Matt. 10:14) and either go to another church or start one of your own. On the other hand, it could be argued that, precisely because this church is so hard to crack, right here is your ministry. It is not an easy decision, and the only way to make it is for your group to decide which offers them more servanthood: doing it on their own and leaving, doing it with the recalcitrants and staying, or doing it with another church where there will also be recalcitrants but where there may be fewer of them. Making that decision will take time and prayer. Reread the end of Chapter 9.

FOURTEEN

How to Keep Your Church Organized

I

There are certain things that must be done if the plan is to be executed.

One, as indicated, the minister must get the right person in the right job at the right time. This means people with initiative. It means people with follow through. If you have those two ingredients, you have a leader. Without them you have a typical "volunteer"—long on talk and short on action.

Two, the minister and leader draw up the plan before the beginning of the calendar, fiscal, or church year. What we want to do in this particular area. How we want to do it. Who will do what, when. They agree. They are together. Each knows what the other wants. If this takes more than one session, take it.

Three, the leader presents the plan to the official board. In writing. Preferably mailed before the meeting. One page. Since each member of the board is doing this for his or her area, all plans should be top quality and should have a good chance of "passing." If there is trouble with any part of a plan, it should be held over to the next meeting. If the suggestion is good it should be incorporated. If it is bad the suggester should be taken out to lunch.

Four, the minister meets with the leader monthly to see that the plan is being executed. They keep each other alert. The minister is the staff assigned to the particular area. The leader is the head of the area. Together they are responsible for, in the cliché, planning the work and working the plan. But it is the minister's job to keep the leader executing. That is what the leader, among others, pays him to do. The buck stops with the minister, not with the leader. If the leader stops executing, the minister should rev him/her up or get another leader. If the minister stops executing, you cannot expect the volunteer leader to rev *him* up. It may happen, and it happens often enough, fortunately, to keep a lot of churches going. But you can't expect it. It's not the leader's job. Therefore if the minister stops executing, he should be fired. He was hired to execute. If he will execute only when someone puts a burr under his saddle blanket, then you don't want that kind of executive running your show. Like any other person in a church, he should get with it or get out.

II

Despite such enthusiasm, however, one of the most serious problems in churches is the congregational copout. You've got the man (it's always a man, even though there are hundreds of ordained women). You're paying him well, or at least reasonably well. Therefore the congregation says it's obviously up to him not only to get it done but to do it.

Not so. As we have seen, you don't hire the minister to do what somebody else could do as well. You hire him to do what somebody else could *not* do as well. You hire him to plan. Sure you hire him to preach and teach. You hire him to visit the sick and counsel the troubled. But others can do those things. Jesus was a layman and he did all of them. Many laymen/laywomen are certainly every bit as equipped to do a minister's traditional roles as he is. Perhaps more equipped.

What they are not equipped to do is to plan. They are not equipped to see the big picture. It's not their job. It's not where they spend their time. It's not where they rise and fall. Jesus had a 3-year plan. He stuck to it. He brought others along with him. That's leadership. That's what a minister is hired to do.

If, however, he doesn't do it, the congregation's job is to insist that he does or to insist that he leave. Somebody has to lift up the big picture. Everybody can preach, teach, visit, counsel. That's the genius of the beloved community. Somebody has to see that everybody does it. And everybody has to see that somebody gets them to do it *if* he isn't getting them to do it on their own.

Every minister, for instance, knows perfectly well where his congregation's weaknesses are. The question is, will he do anything about them? Being as indolent as everyone else, the minister may not unless he is pushed. The congregation doesn't do his job for him. They get him to do his job. Then they work with him to get the job done. Their job is to keep *his* feet to the fire, if necessary, just as his job is to keep *their* feet to the fire. Or, if that metaphor is too "secular," their job is to be a channel of the Spirit for him. His job is to be a channel for them. They in-spire him. He in-spires them. This means that, by golly, you get on your phone and call your minister and say, "Look, we've got a weakness here, and I suggest you think about the following." Or, "Congratulations, that's one of the strongest programs we've ever had at this church, and I just wanted you to know it." Honest praise is an admirable way to keep feet to fires.

III

Having said that, however, the root of the planning problem in churches is accountability.

The minister is really accountable to no one for his performance. Even in denominations with tough polities he is, let's face it, not held accountable. His superior never gives him a performance review based on a checklist. Usually because he has no superior.

And despite what I have just said, virtually no one in the congregation ever holds the minister accountable. There may be a "personnel committee," but as we have seen, they are all the minister's golf partners. And further, although there may be 2–3 close friends who love him enough to criticize him, they may never even have thought of a tough checklist. They are not, unlike the superior, in a position to see the big picture. They may be able to see it, but they are not likely to. Why? It's not their job.

By the same token, the members of the congregation are not held accountable. There is no performance review of any church member in any church in America. It is too "judgmental." It is too "un-Christian."

Not so. Jesus was always reviewing his disciples. Ah, but that was Jesus. All right, we measure ourselves by his standards. They are all there in the New Testament. They are objective. We are all judged by them. They all point to suffering service. *But we refuse to hold ourselves accountable to those standards.* It is not the accountability that is un-Christian. It is the *lack* of accountability.

What we must do is build the accountability in. It's nonsense to leave it to "a man and his God." That would be fine if it worked. But it has obviously not worked, or half the world would not be going to bed hungry.

The first church got very uptight about people who did not live up to what was expected of them as Christians. Members were drummed out regularly. They were called *lapsi*. They lapsed, all right, and they had to work to get back in.

Every church should have an accountability committee. One-half male, one-half female, one-half elected by the official board from its own membership, one-half elected by the official board from the congregation, one-sixth under 18, one-sixth 18–25, one sixth 25–35. One part would deal with members. The other would deal with the minister, supplementing the input of his 2–3 friends who love him enough to criticize him. It would meet monthly. That way it can review 1/12 of the minister's job each month. It can determine if every member is studying, sharing, serving. And it can determine if the minister is inspiring every member to study, share, serve.

If a member is found to be weak in any of the three areas, he can be counseled with by a member of the committee, *who is also weak in one or more of the three areas.* Together they work on ways they can both do better—i.e., have a fuller Christian experience. "Let us consider how to stir up one another to love and good works" (Heb. 10:24). Note that this mutual approach eliminates the pharisaism. For it to work, of course, takes some mature human beings. The accountability committee is not for everyone.

If the minister is found to be weak in any of the three areas, he too can be counseled with, by a member of the committee *who is also weak.* Again they can work together. The minister, incidentally, knows what his weaknesses are. With somebody pressing him on them, he could turn them into strengths.

Of course, it may be that a person, member or minister, feels that the accountability committee is leaning on him or her too hard. In this case, he tells them. If that does no good, he can appeal to the church ombudsman.

One of the perennial problems of churches is that members let disaffection fester. If, however, they knew there was an independent, impartial, neutral fellow Christian specifically designated to hear problems and seek solutions, the creative contributions of all members could be immeasurably enhanced. The ombudsman, elected yearly by the congregation at its annual meeting, takes all the gripes and tries to work them out between the people involved.

Now this individual does not, of course, spring full blown from the head of Zeus. A post like this is not for everyone. It is especially not for the congregation's chief critic (which could be you). It is for a good, strong, supportive man or woman who has been in the congregation a number of years, is deeply religious, lives his or her religion, and has the respect of all. *Every congregation has such a person.* As you read this paragraph, you knew instantly who he or she was in your church. Get the name to the nominating committee. Or, list the job qualifications, have a secret ballot next Sunday, and *the* person in your congregation will have a clear majority.

Now to be sure, even in spite of the ombudsman, the accountability committee is going to get some church members very uptight. Fine.

There are too many people in too many churches who have had a free ride too long. The goal is suffering service. If you don't want to be a suffering servant, then get out of the organization of the Suffering Servant. The virtue of the accountability committee is that it trims down the membership. Only those who mean business are left.

However, no one means business enough. "*All* have sinned and fall short of the glory of God" (Rom. 3:23). This does not mean that we should not do what we can to be suffering servants. It does mean that we will never be suffering servants enough. Therefore we must all be saved, not by accountability committees but by the grace of God.

But how does God's grace happen? An infinite number of ways. "The wind blows where it wills" (John 3:8). All I am arguing for is that one way, particularly for middle-class Americans in the 1970s, is *to do all that we can to become suffering servants* because it may only be then that we will realize we can do *nothing* and that we have to be saved by grace. If the old way of doing nothing and then getting God's grace had worked, that would be one thing. But it has patently not worked. That is why the church no longer cuts it with millions of people—particularly young, poor, black, red, and third-world people. Therefore it is time to try the new way of doing *everything* in our power to realize that it is *not* in our power. That may be the *only* way self-reliant, highly achieving, middle-class Americans can make it. Or, more to the point: the only way grace can make it through them.

> By the grace of God I am what I am. . . . I *worked* harder than any of them, though it was *not* I, but the grace of God which is with me (1 Cor. 15:10).

IV

The classic problem in accountability is that there is no higher body holding the minister and congregation accountable. Virtually every Protestant church in America is able to call its own shots, do its own thing, go its own way. A congregation fails to make it in benevolences? So what? Fails in social action? So what? Fails in getting the Bible read? So what? No heads are going to roll. No jobs are going to be lost. No congregation is going to be dissolved. Nothing is going to happen because you failed to be a suffering servant. It's the same old laissez-faire ball game.

What is needed is top-down *power* in denominations. Individual churches must be forced to toe the line, just as individual states are subordinate to the national state. We fought a war over this in 1861. The trouble with the Protestant church in America is that it has never had a civil war. And that it has never, for some inexplicable reason, learned from America's Civil War.

No, this is not "too Catholic." If you want that kind of power, the argument goes, go back to the Inquisition. You had it then and look what a mess the church made of things. But that isn't the point. The point is not that the federal suggestion is too Catholic but that the current flaccidity is too Protestant. You just cannot have an atomized church if you expect to make it in the 1970s.

The denomination owns the *franchise*. It *sells* the franchise to the local church.

The *conditions* of using the higher judicatory's *name* are as follows:

1. That you will trim your membership by 1/3 within two years (remember: churches are 1/3 committed, 1/3 peripheral, 1/3 out).

2. That you will build nothing that is not matched dollar for dollar with benevolences; that is how you buy your franchise.

3. That you will submit a plan of action for the higher judicatory's approval.

4. That that plan must be based on the most powerful image we have of Jesus, namely, as Suffering Servant or on another image which you can demonstrate to be of equal power.

5. That that plan must contain certain minimal standards of membership.

6. That those standards must reflect the first church's

kerygma, koinonia, and *diakonia.*

7. That you will set up a 5-year plan, at the end of which you will match every dollar you spend on yourself, excluding debt retirement, with a dollar for benevolences.
8. That you will set up a subsequent 5-year plan, at the end of which you will also be matching every dollar you spend on your mortgage with a dollar for benevolences.
9. That failure to match operating and benevolences in 5 years and mortgage and benevolences in another 5 will result in loss of your franchise and you can no longer use the name of the denomination.
10. That failure to submit an annual plan will also mean loss of your franchise.
11. That you will send your minister to the head office to be trained, annually, in how to push, pull, yank, persuade, call, goad his church to meet the denomination's servanthood objectives.
12. That if he won't come or if he won't report or if his reports show a steady "loss" of servanthood, then you will *lose* your franchise. You can call yourself whatever you want, but you can't use the name of this denomination.

Admittedly these conditions are tough, but the condition of the American church is tougher. It is sick unto death. If the old way of ragged individualism had worked, that would be one thing. But it has patently not worked. Every church is out there doing its own potty little thing, and it has lost the kids, lost the blacks, lost the executives, lost the third world. The church is in desperate shape. It needs a structural revolution to get it into shape. And that does *not* mean COCU. Not as it is presently structured (see Appendix 2). It means each denomination doing what it was supposed to do all along. Namely, whip its troops into shape and give the world some stunning symbols of suffering service.

FIFTEEN

How to Be Organized by the Spirit

What does the church do that no other organization does? It might appear that the church studies, and that that is its uniqueness. But the school studies. The college studies. The Rockefeller Institute studies. And they all study better than the church.

It might appear that the church shares, and that that is its uniqueness. But people share in group therapy. They share in counseling. They share in families. And they often share more deeply there than in the church.

Or it might appear that the church serves, and that that is its uniqueness. But the political party serves. The corporation serves. The welfare department serves. And they often serve far better than the church.

What does the church do that other organizations don't do? Yes, the church studies, shares, *and* serves. That suggests some uniqueness. But the school, for example, studies. It is beginning to share. And it is even beginning to serve.

What makes the church unique is the Spirit. It is the Spirit that moves the church to think. It is the Spirit that moves the church to feel. It is the Spirit that moves the church to act. Now this is not to say that the Spirit is limited to the church. Surely the Spirit can be in the school, the home, the political party. It is only to say that the church is limited to the Spirit. If there is no Spirit, then there is no church. But if there is no church, there may still be the Spirit.

I

How do you *know* it's the Spirit? It could be simply good thinking. It could be good feeling. It could be good acting.

You know it's the Spirit because you are overpowered. The church is a power-broker. Yes, you can be overpowered in plenty of other organizations. But you *are* overpowered in the church. If you aren't overpowered, then it isn't the church. We have plenty of people in churches. Not so many in the church.

"The Spirit immediately drove him out into the wilderness" (Mark 1:12). It was an example of power. He had thought, felt, done before. He had studied, shared, served. But then it was all put together in the first overpowering experience of his life.

Ah, but that was Jesus. He was exceptional. Of course. But what about the others? The experience was replicated for them. Peter, Paul, James, John, Mary. They were unexceptional. Indeed, they were distinguished by nothing so much as their ordinariness. They were like us.

Ah, but it happened suddenly, and I am not a "sudden" kind of person. Things happen to me gradually. Do they? Were you married gradually? Did you graduate gradually? Did you get promoted gradually? On the one hand, yes, of course. You worked. It took months, years. But on the other hand the event itself happened in a matter of moments. And that is the way it was with Jesus. He trained for 30 years. Then it happened. So if we say that the Spirit overpowers us in a moment, we are saying it has likely been overpowering us for years.

O.K. So the Spirit comes gradually as well as suddenly. How do I know it is coming? What if I have no sudden or gradual experiences to prove it was there all along? But you have. They are happening all the time. You find yourself doing something you wouldn't normally do. You find yourself feeling something you wouldn't normally feel. You find yourself thinking something you wouldn't normally think. You read the Bible, for instance. You share your life. You give yourself. It has to be the Spirit because it couldn't be you. It is not the kind of thing *you* would normally do.

But why the *Spirit?* Surely the atheist gives himself. Surely the Buddhist shares his feelings. Surely the Hindu reads his Scripture. None of them attributes what they do to the Spirit. Fine. Let them attribute it to whatever they want. You attribute it to the Spirit.

But do I? Granted I am not an atheist, Buddhist, or Hindu. I still may not attribute my overpowering experiences to the Spirit. I could attribute them to the logical outcome of my work. I could attribute them to coincidence. I could attribute them to luck. Why the Spirit?

Because you had your experiences in community. Apart from the church you wouldn't read the Bible. You wouldn't share yourself. You wouldn't give your life. You *might.* But the chances are excellent you wouldn't. The chances are you didn't. *Did* you look for the meaning of your life in the Bible apart from the church? *Did* you share the meaning of your life apart from the church? *Did* you give yourself apart from the church? You may have. But then again you may not.

What happens in the church that may not happen elsewhere has always been attributed to the Spirit. The Spirit *is* what you do because of the church that you would not normally do. If the church simply blesses what you are doing, good as that may be, it is not enough. When you join the church, it has to make a difference. You have to change. That change, gradually and suddenly, *is* the Spirit.

It is this change that is the power. You go to school and are educated. But are you changed? You go to group therapy and are improved. But are you changed? You join a political party and are confirmed in your judgments. But are you changed?

Now you *may* be. It is the height of arrogance to limit the Spirit to the church. "The wind blows where it wills," Jesus said (John 3:8). The Spirit is free. It is not bound to the church. You may be changed by any number of organizations in society. But you *will* be changed by the church or it isn't the church. "If any one is in Christ," Paul said, "he is a *new* creation" (2 Cor. 5:17).

Let's be frank. The church, like any institution, often gets in the way of the very thing it is trying to do. "First the spirit builds its house," Emerson said, "and then the house confines the spirit."[1] The church kills the Spirit. It blocks the power. It prevents the change. It is content when it should be dissatisfied. It is satisfied when it should be upset.

Nevertheless, the little white building on the prairie houses the most powerful organization in the history of the world. It is more powerful than the White House. More powerful than the Kremlin. More powerful than the Houston Space Center. Each of these is powerful, make no mistake. But they don't change lives, not in the spiritual sense. The church does that. And churches prevent its being done.

Fortunately, however, the church has more going for it than itself. It has the Spirit. The Spirit *is* what the church has going for it. Yes, the White House has the Spirit going for it. Yes, the Kremlin and Houston have the Spirit going for them. You can't limit the Spirit. "For God so loved the *world*" (John 3:16). What the church has that these other power-brokers lack is a total inability to do *anything* significant apart from the Spirit. The church exists because of the Spirit. It can do nothing apart from the Spirit. "Apart from me you can do *nothing*" (John 15:5). Houston can do anything. It doesn't rely on the Spirit for its power. Indeed, it is precisely a monument to man's ability to do his own thinking. The White House and the Kremlin are monuments to our ability to do our own acting. The Menninger Clinic is a monument to our ability to do our own feeling.

And that is precisely what the church is not. It can't think. It can't feel. It can't act. It can't study. It can't share. It can't serve. Not on its own. Whenever it tries, it may or may not get into trouble. The point is, it just doesn't perform very well. It can't think as well as the school. It can't feel as well as the clinic. And it can't act as well as the political party.

But when the Spirit gets the church thinking, that's power. When the Spirit gets the church feeling, that's power. When the Spirit gets the church acting, that's power. Indeed, the Spirit *is* what *over*powers our thinking. It is what *over*powers our feeling. It is what *over*powers our acting.

Who could possibly think that Jesus is the Christ apart from the Spirit? The Spirit *is* what gets us to think that thought. "No man can say that Jesus is Lord but by the spirit" (1 Cor. 12:3). A young man got up and said Jesus was the most important thing in his life. He said it to a church.

Who could possibly share the deep places in his life apart from the Spirit? The Spirit *is* what gets us to feel that emotion. A woman called to say, "Thank you for the most beautiful experience in our lives." She said it to a church.

Who could possibly give himself, in love to the uttermost, apart from the Spirit? The Spirit *is* what gets us to do that. A man stood up and said he was dumfounded by all the money he was giving away. He said it to a church.

How do you *know* it's the Spirit? Because *you* aren't doing it. It's being done through you, not by you. You're overpowered. "You shall receive *power* when the Holy Spirit has come upon you" (Acts 1:8).

II

All right, how do you *get* the Spirit? How you know it is one thing. How you get it is another.

You don't get it. It gets you. That sounds glib, of course, but consider. If the Spirit is so powerful that it overpowers you, clearly it is in control and you aren't. "This is not your own doing," wrote a stunned early Christian. "It is the gift of God" (Eph. 2:8). "You did not choose me," Jesus said, ". . . I chose you" (John 15:15). There is nothing we can do to get the Spirit. The Spirit gets us.

You can keep all the commandments. You can obey all the laws. You can do all the rituals. And that's fine if that's your style. But don't expect it to deliver the Spirit. The Spirit cannot be bound to the church. And the Spirit cannot be bound to your way of bringing the Spirit. "Since all have sinned," Paul wrote, "and fall short of the glory of God, they are justified by his grace as a gift" (Rom. 3:23–24). Not as a reward. "It was not because you were more in number than any other people," the Deuteronomist wrote, "but it is because the Lord loves you" (Deut. 7:7–8). That was all. You don't get it. It gets you. It was precisely the Pharisees, who obeyed all the laws, who did not get the Spirit. And it was precisely the street people who broke the laws who did (Matt. 21:31).

You don't get the Spirit. The spirit gets you. But there's more to it than that. We have said that you know the Spirit in community. You also *get* the spirit in community. It is not a condition, simply an aid. But it is a powerful aid. "Since you are eager for manifestations of the *spirit,*" Paul wrote the Corinthians, "strive to excel in building up the *church*" (1 Cor. 14:12). No Spirit—no church. And now we are close, although not there, to no church—no Spirit.

"Help build up the church." You can't make it alone as a Christian. The power just isn't there. We need the church as the power-broker. Buddha could sit under a tree and become enlightened. The Hindu can contemplate the other world doing yoga. To be sure, the Christian can pray and read and think alone. But in the final analysis the Christian has to have other people to experience the full power of his religion.

Something is happening in the church that is not happening under the tree. This is not to say the tree is not important. For many it is very important. Even Jesus withdrew to pray. But Jesus began it all with 12 average people. So average that one of them couldn't believe that the Spirit was happening and he quit. Jesus knew something was going on among many people that you couldn't get alone. That couldn't get you alone. Even he had to have other people.

Why? It's impossible to say. It can only be experienced. No, that's not a copout. It's simply an admission that language is limited. The Spirit isn't, but the language is. That's why the New Testament writers could never make up their minds what to call the church. They called it "the body of Christ" (1 Cor. 12:27). They called it "the houschold of God" (Eph. 2:19). The called it the "Israel of God" (Gal. 6:16). They called it "God's beloved" (Rom. 1:7). But nothing quite caught the experience called "church."

Never ask a person to describe his church to you. He will fall all over himself trying to. If, that is, it's a church. If it isn't a church he'll be able to describe it very well. But if it's a church, if it's spirit-ual, all he will be able to say is that he doesn't know where the Spirit will strike next. The stronger the description, then, the weaker the church. But when a person stumbles, when he becomes inarticulate about his church, not from ignorance but from fullness, when all he or she can do is what the man did at the beginning of John, and say, "Come and see" (John 1:46), then you know something's happening. Then you know there are a lot of overpowered people there who have been dumfounded by the Spirit. If you want the Spirit, find the church.

Now let's be honest again. There are a lot of things that turn people off about churches. And justifiably so. The church spends more on itself than on others. It refuses to spread the Good News. It is hardly overpowering on Sunday morning, let alone at any other time. The church kills the very thing it is trying to grow. It destroys what it is trying to create. It is as pharisaical as the Pharisees.

Maybe that's why Paul said, if you want the Spirit, build the church. Get in there and give it a hand. Criticize it, yes. But criticize it with love. Build it up. Don't tear it down. There are plenty of people who will do that. What the church needs, what you need if you want the Spirit, what the Spirit needs, is people who want to be overpowered. People who don't have all the answers. People who need each other.

That's quite an admission, that we need each other. It has a dynamic, a power of its own. If you want the Spirit, build the church. Paul realized that when people needed each other, that was a chance for the Spirit. That *was* the Spirit. You couldn't say it, mind you. But you could feel it. And the feeling *was* the Spirit. "The Spirit himself intercedes for us with sighs too deep for words" (Rom. 8:26).

But is that all? Just a few vaguely defined feelings? What about miracles? What about ecstasies? What about speaking in tongues? Aren't they how you really get the Spirit? Fine, if that's your style. But they're not essential. "Paul plays down speaking with tongues," writes a New Testament expert. "The criterion of the extraordinary was . . . irrelevant."[2] What was relevant was the feeling that you needed other people if you were going to be overpowered.

And what if I'm not an emotional person? But you are, you know. You really are. Even the most driving executive is emotional. His problem is that he lives on only two levels, thinking and doing, when he should be getting off them regularly to feeling. He has to be in control of his business or he gets fired. Therefore he erroneously but understandably feels he has to be in control of his emotions or he will fail as a person. Or she will. One of the great things women's lib has done for us is to remind men that they can feel. And women that they can think. And both that they can be in the church. *Be* the church.

An 8-year-old went to the Museum of Natural History with her Brownie troop. They came to an exhibit entitled, "Can Man Survive?" Asked afterward, "Well, can he?" she answered, "I don't know about him, but we're working on it in Brownies."[3]

III

Finally, once you get the Spirit, how do you *keep* it? It's a perennial question. The popular idea of the Spirit is that of an emotion-laden experience which washes off with the next bath. But that, of course, isn't what happens at all. You don't keep the Spirit. The Spirit keeps you. Again it sounds glib but is anything but. You find yourself doing the most extraordinary things. They are outside the ordinary run of your life. Just as you found yourself thinking thoughts you would not normally think and feeling emotions you would not normally let yourself feel, so you're also dumfounded to find yourself doing things you never dreamed you would do.

No, they're not necessarily big things. You may not be driven by the Spirit to save the world. But, like Jesus, you are driven by the

Spirit. You find yourself doing all sorts of things you would never have done on your own. That, of course, is just the point. You aren't on your own. You are in the grip of the Spirit.

You may very well, for instance, find yourself talking about things you wouldn't normally talk about. Not that you know what you're saying. And not that you can say it very well. Because we can never catch the Spirit. The Spirit *is* what we cannot catch. But there you are talking about some friendly strangers you bumped into who have become the strange friends who are your church.

> I just couldn't accept what I saw happening at [church] as being real. Like . . . how in the world did all these phonies manage to find each other? Now I seldom pray but what I thank God for all these beautiful people.

But, of course, there's more to the talk than that. Gradually you find yourself being inarticulate not only about the people who are the church but about the man behind the church. Certainly you never dreamed that *you* would be talking about *Jesus.* But it's happening. That's how you are kept by the Spirit.

You may also find your talent being used by the church. No, it may not be a big thing. But it is a big thing for you. After all, it is you, and you are being used. You never dreamed your talent would end up here. You are a "helper" (1 Cor. 12:28). You are an "administrator" *(idem).* You give "service" (Rom. 12:7). You do "acts of mercy" *(idem).* Nothing spectacular. But you. You're not another Paul. You won't set the world on fire. But you are you. And he knew this. That is why he made a point of saying there is a place here for you. So it isn't just what you wouldn't normally do, but what you would normally do only in a different place with different people. That's how the change takes place, the power. That's how the Spirit keeps you.

There are other ways. Here you are, the guy or gal who could never show emotion, and you find yourself showing it. And what is showing emotion but giving yourself? Have you been surprised to see people crying in church? We should be surprised if we do *not* see people crying in church. The church are the people who give their sadness and joy to each other. "If one member suffers," Paul wrote, "all suffer together. If one member is honored, all rejoice together" (1 Cor. 12:26). The Spirit is that overpowering.

And it's not just Sunday morning. That's only the top of the iceberg. What goes on throughout the church's life is this overpowering feeling that we are here to give ourselves to one another, to reveal ourselves that much, to "bear one another's burdens" (Gal. 6:2) *that much.* Therefore anything, *anything,* that gets in the way of our giving ourselves to each other is inappropriate in churches. No, this does not mean that churches should avoid controversy. Jesus even provoked it. Often the most giving thing we can do is to share where we really are, not only with ourselves but one another.

What it does mean is that the Spirit is so powerful that it can take people who differ on a great many things and make them into one body for Christ. "That they may all be one," Jesus said (John 17:21). And it's staggering when you think about it. Because he was talking about Jews and non-Jews, aggressors and defenders, colonializers and colonialized, in a word, enemies. "That they may all be one." And that's been the breathtaking, the overpowering message of the church, that most speechless of institutions, ever since. Which means it has been what church people have found themselves doing. That's how the Spirit keeps us.

But there is, of course, "a still more excellent way," as Paul put it (1 Cor. 12:31), to keep the Spirit. And that is the way of love to the uttermost, giving yourself so much for someone else that you not only give your emotions but even your life. This is the purest form of the Spirit. It is the most powerful. Obviously we are not going to give ourselves that much. Therefore it has to be the Spirit, since it can't be us. We are overpowered. We are speechless before our actions. We are dumfounded at what we see ourselves doing.

This is the meaning behind Jesus' most radical statements. "Turn the other cheek." "Go the second mile." "Love your enemies." "Deny yourself." "Take up your cross." The Spirit, he was saying—more accurately *God*—is so powerful that you find yourself doing what you would never do, namely, allow yourself to be given for another.

Do you remember reading of the priest in the Nazi concentration camp who gave himself for the other man?[4] The man had been selected to die when the priest broke ranks and offered to be killed in his place. The man is alive and in Poland. The priest has been made a saint.

Now, to be sure, it may never come to that for us. But there is a sense in which it always comes to that. The Spirit is that overpowering. We are continually being challenged to give ourselves that much. And it is the church that issues the challenge—*through* which the challenge *is* issued. That is why churches give away far more than they spend on themselves. No, no one in the church dies because of that. But there is a sense in which there *is* that much giving. Because a lot of things the church may have wanted to do for itself *will* have to die. They just are not that important when matched against Christ's radical standard of love to the uttermost.

It is this progression of the Spirit which is overpowering. It is why the martyrs could sing on their way to their deaths. It is why an incredulous world could watch while "the pernicious superstition," as the Roman historian Tacitus called it, grew with every new Christian who gave his or her life in love to the uttermost. A conversation. A book. An administrative job. A laugh. A tear. These are how the Spirit, strange as it may seem, keeps us. But then there is this even stranger progression to love to the uttermost. And that is the *most* powerful thing in the world. It *can't* be those who give themselves. It *has* to be the Spirit.

I spent a night with Bob and Nancy in Boston. There had been a conversation. Bob had been talking with one of his colleagues about, of all things, the church. And then they had called me because they wanted me to come out and continue the conversation with them and some others. And I, of course, didn't want to go because I had things to do and Boston is a long way. So it was hardly love to the uttermost. But there was a power pulling me. And I went.

And there we all were, 30 or so of us in a room in a church. An Episcopal church. And the wind began to blow. And when the wind begins to blow in an Episcopal church, watch out. Because the Spirit can be very powerful indeed. And suddenly at the end of the evening, there was Nancy, praying. And it wasn't what she said but the way she said it. Just a sentence or two. And then she choked up. And she stopped. And person after person picked it up. They prayed. Can you imagine Episcopalians praying without their prayer books? The man next to me prayed for his daughter who had had an operation. And I put my hand out. And we were close. And then another man prayed —for me. And a wonderful older woman prayed for their minister. And another. And another. And then it was over. And there wasn't a dry eye in the place. It was unbelievable. The vestry. New England. People were hugging each other. It was overpowering. It was the Spirit. "The wind blows where it wills. . . ." It was the church.

Appendices

1

LETTERS AND COMMENTS CON AND PRO

Con

Bob,

There are two kinds of religion. God's plan, as God a spirit, lead [*sic*] by intelligent men. The natural religion, as God a myth, lead [*sic*] by selfish men.

Time is coming to an impasse. I know that you know, that this is an anti-Christ church. This makes you a wolf in sheeps [*sic*] clothing. I would like to choke you. What you have built on God's foundation does show to the entire community. This church has an anti-Christ label. I don't like having the Presbyterian Church degraded! Would you convert from Saul to Paul? We need you desperately.

Psalms 103:17

P.S.

If you will understand Psalms 103:17 through the enlightment [sic] of God the spirit, you will see that your family has only damnation in the future. Because you are a totally selfish person you are hating and hurting everyone including yourself. To save yourself and anyone who may follow you, convert now to God the spirit. As you grow in accordance with God the spirit, your mind will mature from an adolescent to a mature mind.

Call me, or send a note, so that I will know that you have read this.

Pro

Here are the papers you asked us to review and complete if we were planning to join St. Luke's.

Much as I'd hate to jeopardize my future with your congregation by admitting any doubts or reservations, I feel I must admit a few. . . .

For instance, maybe I'm not ready for such total commitment. And I suspect part of the problem is money. (Where one's heart, his treasure, etc.—I know, I know.) Sacrificial giving, tithing and all that; I know, I've been there too, if only as a member of the Every Member Canvass Committee.

But another problem is involvement. Not just in the tiny community surrounding the church, but in Metro Minneapolis . . . and the ghetto . . . the country as a whole, the world at large.

Of course, this *is* what Christianity is all about, but yours is the first church I've been this near that actually seems to *practice* all the rules. Tho, perhaps, in somewhat less-than-conventional fashion!

As an ordained elder (too-soon-ordained, I've long felt) I can find no fault with the system, approach and/or commitment of St. Luke members . . . but I can foresee a small problem in *my* involvement. (Not my wife's; she'll go all the way, but business and personal problems may present a not-so-small conflict for me.)

On the other hand, I resisted coming to this area for a long time. And once I arrived, I learned that "everything" around here is new and different. Not only the weather, but the people . . . not just my job, but the company for which I work . . . the neighborhood where we found a temporary home . . . and the home itself.

So why should a "new" church bother me?

Well, for one thing, I've always been associated with the more traditional—if stuffy—forms of Presbyterianism. Separation of not only church and state, but church and most things outside the physical plant of the church as well. Politics? Never! Peace movement?

Well—as long as it's quiet and orderly, doesn't take too much time and doesn't upset anyone. Drugs, prison reform, inner city problems? Of course, but we must keep them at a distance. . . .

And I keep remembering St. Augustine. (Soon, Lord, soon . . . but not just yet!)

Job and home and family and relatives and personal problems and activities first. Then we'll think of others. Trust in the Lord, of course; but meanwhile, better concentrate on that little nest-egg for the future. . . .

A favorite sermon theme of a minister I once knew "back east" concerned the three things early Christians had in common:

> they were always happy
> they were absolutely fearless
> they were always in trouble.

Maybe it's time to get into trouble.

Maybe it's time to put my faith to work, to take a chance, to get involved with some of the more significant essentials. . . . And I'm willing to try, if you and the rest of St. Luke's are ready to give me (us) the opportunity.

Thank you.

Con

As a result of Robert Hudnut's sermon on October 29, we do not feel at this time that we want to make a pledge for 1968. We have made a pledge each and every year up to this time.

Pro

After thinking about this letter through three loads of wash, preparing lunch, and pumping up the tires on the bikes, I'm not sure how much sense is left in it. Thinking about things too long sometimes jumbles them up. But I have an overwhelming need to tell you how much St. Luke is changing my life.

Four years ago, when we wandered in because it was the closest Presbyterian church to where we lived, you all made me furious. I should have been alerted at the time—anything that affected my emotions that much was getting to me, even if it was a negative reaction. I couldn't believe that the church could ask so much of people. After all, I had small children and Sunday morning was the only hour of peace I had all week. It was by no means peaceful! I don't know when I stopped rebeling and started moving with the tide—I guess that process isn't complete even yet.

A lot of tiny incidents suddenly began to add up to make me realize what was happening. In another city we were sitting around the dinner table when someone said, "The church seems to be a big part of your life." My father, whom I see once or twice a year, stopped in town briefly on his way home from a business trip. Most of the evening was spent talking about his church and mine. Last night at a dinner party, with people we don't know well, we talked for ages about God and the church.

Two years ago it was impossible for me to witness—now it is impossible for me not to. It comes up everywhere, coffee parties, family reunions. I used to think that people who talked about their religion a lot were slightly strange and embarrassing—why doesn't that worry me any more? When I think how vulnerable I have allowed myself to become, it is terrifying—but it doesn't seem to stop me.

St. Luke has stretched me so much. I find myself doing things that were beyond me before. The incredible support you all give me allows me to take the risk of failing. These are not great, important tasks but for me they were a lot—and I found I could do them. I come to church knowing that these people care about me no matter what; and I leave renewed and refreshed, and ready for another challenge.

I'm so grateful that my children can grow up in the midst of this group of people—a sense of God can't help but creep into their very bones with exposure.

Con

I would rather talk to you in person but knowing how such good intentions get put off, I'm going to put it down in letter form right now and still try to get together with you.

I do not come to church to hear the statements of the other worshippers concerning their beliefs. I think that religion is a private and a very individualistic thing and oddly enough although our individual beliefs vary, we all get tremendous inspiration from your service. But when each individual starts describing his own beliefs, it becomes disharmonious and contentious. The place for this is in the small groups where it really works, not, in my opinion, in the Sunday worship service. If I liked the kind of thing we seem to be moving toward I would have long ago joined a Unitarian or a Universalist church. But I do not consider myself a minister and I do not consider my fellow members of the congregation ministers. I do not expect to preach to them and I do not expect them to preach to me. The two-part sermon is of value and inspiration to me only insofar as part one goes. In part two we invariably quickly stray from "driving the point home" and have some meaningless and some academic questions about why we are there. I know why I'm there and frankly I guess I don't have the patience to hear those who stand up inquiring about why they are there.

Sincerely,

Pro

Yesterday, the 19th, we attended worship at St. Luke. My wife said many people were crying tears of joy as they left. I didn't notice—my vision was blurred!

Our worship experiences at St. Luke began about twelve years ago. We attend six or eight times a year when visiting relatives. We have found worship at St. Luke a treasured privilege.

At present, we are contemplating a move which would not allow us to worship at St. Luke more than once or twice a year. The thought of separation is painful. We feel like our major source of renewal would be cut off. You have opened the Spirit of Wholeness to us. Thank you for opening and Being.

                                                    In His Name,

Con

With regret, we write to tell you that we no longer can plan to attend St. Luke as members of the church. We pray that this move will not sever our friendships with the many sincere people at St. Luke, and we look forward to occasionally sharing in your worship and fellowship in the future.

There are always several reasons for a decision such as this . . . the greatest of these relates to our personal spiritual needs, and is the only valid reason for us to consider a change which grieves us as much as this does. As we have considered other factors, it seems that this is the only course open to us.

As individuals, we find our own way to God, and our way to love Him and serve Him. The St. Luke way is so good for so many, but we have been like square pegs trying to fit round holes; it is not our way.

We are enclosing our pledge for September and October. Our lack of employment and financial situation during the summer have made a revision of our pledge for the year a necessity. We regret that we cannot meet our original pledge.

We thank you for the help and strength we have derived from our association with you and the members of St. Luke.

Sincerely yours,

Pro

To the congregation on the day of his joining:

My faith has always been like going out on the ice and at the first sign of cracking coming back. Ninety-five per cent of the churches I've ever been in—they'd all be behind you, pulling you back. Ninety-five per cent of the people at St. Luke would be in the water.

Con

I feel that the young lady's little talk [on the invasion of Cambodia] was in very bad taste.I assume the objective of the talk was to exhort the members of the congregation to express themselves to their elected representatives on the current controversial issues: particularly the war in Southeast Asia. However she spent most of her time mouthing irrational left-wing cliches such as "tools of the administration." In so doing, she failed to accomplish the objective and merely irritated people.

In contrast, the girl at the second service accomplished the objective with a very intelligent talk.

If the church service is going to be used to express extreme views of its members then let's give someone from the ultra-right an opportunity to speak next week. However, I would prefer such discussions to go on outside of the church service.

I dearly love St. Luke church and what it stands for, but I think there is a danger that we are so liberal, that we feed on each other's liberality and reinforce each other's thinking. Let's be liberal in the true sense, and hear all sides of the questions.

Pro

WHY I'M GOING TO JOIN THE CHURCH

I've definitely decided to, but I'm still not sure why. I hesitated because the church, for me, had so long represented organized religion, which I detest. The fact that I could now take communion didn't phase me much, because I feel I can take communion at home—with friends or just alone—and have it mean as much if not more.

There really wasn't any good reason for joining. I could take part in social action, and still come to the services. What would be missing?

For one, I'd probably miss the feeling of alliance. There's a difference between that and brotherhood. Brotherhood you feel everyone is everyone's brother. But alliance, you're all there, united in one cause, for one reason. The cause is humanity, and the reason is Jesus.

For example, at Woodstock, there was brotherhood. But if you met someone else who was there, you can talk about it, and that's as far as it goes. But if you talk to someone that goes to your church—at least I've found this true for St. Luke—man, you've really got something in common. There are all kinds of things you can find out about somebody just by knowing what church he goes to.

What I mean is, and we'll take St. Luke for an example, you ask one question, "So you agree our church should get so involved?" And depending on the answer, you can get a really good rap session going.

In my experience, when I've had a good rap with someone, no matter whether we agree or not, I go away liking the person much better. In that way, you get the brotherhood along with the alliance.

As for me, if this church wasn't up to its neck in social action, I wouldn't join it, alliance or no! I'm sick and tired of this huge organization just sitting around looking holy. The church I join will be active or you can forget it.

By a Member of the 9th Grade Confirmation Class

Con

First of all please don't think of this letter as being critical but hopefully constructive as far as my thoughts are concerned. For a long time you have preached for social action and criticized those who did not participate as actively as you may have thought they should.

Nobody likes the war with all the destruction that takes place and the suffering and death that goes on. At least now steps are being taken to bring our boys home.

To me, Bob, something is missing on going to church on Sunday. Maybe sometime you could give us a little encouragement—talk about some of the good things that are happening in this world. Give the congregation a pat on the back for the good job they are doing —not that we can't do better.

Please accept this letter in the right way and now I selfishly feel better about expressing some of my views to you.

Warmest regards,

Pro

As I told you that morning I was sort of in a state of shock at just the physical change of the church itself, but it was interesting. Perhaps I'm too traditional to handle that right now—I don't know. I didn't feel as though I could fit into it at all. I've become quite a conservative in many ways, but also thinking progressively.

But I did see something there that fascinated me. I remember you used to talk about trying to find some excitement in the church for others and drawing it out of the congregation. (I'm sure that's not exactly what you said, but it was something like that.) Speaking as just a one-hour visitor—I think you've got it! And I'm excited about it! From what I could see and feel, those people are excited about what's happening. I think it's terrific!

And that's what I wanted to say.

Your friend,

Con

I have some thoughts to share with you which I express largely for selfish reasons but also because I care for St. Luke and for what the congregation aspires to be.

I've heard nothing but praise for St. Luke. In fact, I'm almost certain that praise is expected. In the context of suburban churches altogether, I suppose it's justified. My own response to St. Luke is one of progressive disappointment.

The first Sunday morning worship experience with St. Luke members was exciting. The initial visual impression was at once encouraging: modest building, homemade accoutrements, old pews, folding chairs, circular seating—evidence of priorities. Men and women at the door with bulletins impressed me. Liturgy and sermon represented better theology than I had heard in a long time. The test came at the end of the service. Greetings came unsolicited., I had been looking for community in a congregation and seemed to find it here. I ignored doubts about whether any people committed to the American Dream could accept Christ's mandates and decided to seek membership.

Doubts began to surface when I joined others in a winter group workshop. I found us playing a game which drew upon member competitiveness and profit motives, instead of encouraging the supportive and facilitative relationships essential to groups. As a specialist in human communication, I left with mingled feelings of alienation and disgust, while still holding out the hope that St. Luke staff and congregates [sic] were well-intentioned, at least.

There followed a growing confrontation with the images of corporation executive (realized or aspired to) and corporation executive's wife. The American Dream was indeed there. Christ's message received lip service and token response. Sermons remained inspiring for their content and implications. They evaporated in front of the pulpit. Great liberal causes swept some up in excitement and self congratulation. Their self-serving character was exposed by the GMF party "in the plush offices of . . ." while at the same time there was the rest of the world and Christ ministering among them somewhere.

More than intellectual, my criticism is deeply personal. Not for years have I become so defensive, so downright hostile, in the presence of a group of people. Their *idols* and their *social norms* provide no place for me, and indeed they deny me. I came with gifts to share, humble as they are; and I announced some of them. But the response, if it came, was from another source, not from or to where I was. I said a lot of words to some people, but there was no communication.

I've shrunk away in self preservation. I come on Sunday morning for what the sermon brings, and I participate superficially in congregational tasks. But it seems inevitable that I will leave.

Regretfully,

Pro

I'd like to express my gratitude for the positive influence our association with St. Luke has had on our lives. Why it has taken this long is beyond me, particularly when we seem to spout off about our great church to most anyone we come in contact with.

I fought joining St. Luke when we did, but my husband felt so strongly about it and the idea of doing it as a unit that I quit resisting. I resisted because I just couldn't accept what I saw happening at St. Luke as being real. Like . . . how in the world did all these phonies manage to find each other? Now I seldom pray but what I thank God for all the beautiful people at St. Luke.

We have talked frequently about our changed set of values since moving to Minnesota and tried to explain it away as Midwestern friendliness, the birth of our children, etc., etc., but we now know that it was nothing less than our contact with St. Luke.

Con

It is with great reluctance that we have chosen to find a new church home after many years at St. Luke.

I cannot leave without thanking you. Your words have always been thought-provoking and challenging. Particularly we appreciate the strong church education our children received in communicants classes and the great joys of worship in music.

Although we feel we can better find and serve God in another environment, we have great devotion for St. Luke and you, and do wish you all the best.

Pro

I want to thank all of you beautiful people for letting me find something more in God and people.

Your retreat opened my eyes very deeply into the world of God and love like I have never before felt or experienced.

Someday, very soon, I would like very dearly to become a part of your church, your faith, your group, and you.

I have gone to other churches, but none offer what you are offering.

After talking Saturday night about your church, and its way of being, I felt I could and would express myself to God in your church.

All I can say is that you are beautiful people, and I can never thank you enough for accepting me as you did.

From my love, to your love,

SOME COMMENTS—*CON*

Is it true they ask you for your W-2 Form before you join?

I'm leaving the church. The kids are taking over and showing love films.

That worship service could have been held in City Hall.

St. Luke? That's not even a church.

I think you are leading people away from God, mainly in the worship service. I use the church service as a retreat. I'm selfish enough to want God to myself. This is where I get my strength to go on—*away* from the problems of the world.

I shudder when they bring out the guitars.

What the hell's he doing this week?

Telephone call to neighboring Presbyterian Church:
"Is this Bob Hudnut's church?"
"No."
"Well, in that case, what time are your services?"

SOME COMMENTS—*PRO*

This is the only church I know where an hour after the service the parking lot is still full.

Letter from a college freshman:
  "The cool thing is that I am O.K. and open to the possibilities. St. Luke did so much for me. Bye now. Love you unconditionally."

Since I moved to the Twin Cities with my family in November of '65, the most significant impact that has occurred on my life and probably on the life of my family has been St. Luke Church.

I am changed because of this church.

I come to see the smiles on the faces of the people.

This is the only church we've ever come back to.

It's the first time I've ever wanted to go to church on Sunday because I was afraid I might miss something.

I laid them all out on the spot. Nobody, but nobody, criticizes St. Luke.

We really feel we've been reborn, that all roads were leading to this church.

Con

Written on the Back of a Peace Program Pledge Card:
"I have decided it has come to a point, as I said last June, where
it is time to rebel against the deplorable and unrealistic conditions
of St. Luke's physical plant. I will be glad to pay for paint, floor
covering or toward a softener, but no more on pledges of this sort."

Pro

Good morning Bob,

From your late night small group. We missed your face, shoes, hair, socks, etc. May your day reap many wondrous reaps. Let it all hang out. We'll see you next month, hopefully sooner. If this note sounds bad it's because it is. And if it is it's because it's so late.

Signing off,

2
OFFICIAL BOARD MINUTES

MINUTES OF THE SESSION MEETING

Tuesday, February 15, 1972

Old Folk S. D. Geckeler, Merrill Donoho, Dave Heegaard, Jim Littlejohn, George Klein, David Bell, Lynn Cox and Bob Hudnut welcomed new folk: Lila Cargill, Barb Ellenberger, Carol Thomas and Lucy Hartwell.

Mary Bell and Ford Campbell were "playing" at the high school.

Following prayer, the preaching minister discussed session ground rules including the strong, yet unwritten rule regarding the lack of structure.

Following that a supply of stone tablets were delivered to each member. They were called the St. Luke Management Plan. They outlined in great detail the bureaucratic superstructure which makes St. Luke perk. Each session member was given his own tablet outlining his specific area of accountability. It was indicated that chisels and hammers would be available and revisions could indeed be made at later small meetings between "staff" persons and elders in charge.

This author was charged with keeping records of all happenings. Two orders were given:

1. Get all data down.
2. Do it in a fashion meaningful to the group.

At this point the old folk reported.

Lynn Cox reported on the great work of her committee. It included:

1. A successful Social Service Sunday thrust.
2. The start up of a newsletter to include a calendar of social service events written by Al Mahannah.
3. The compilation of a master list inventory telling where the bodies are buried and what they're doing in the area of Social Service.
4. The reviewing of new program suggested at the Social Service Sunday thrust.

It was suggested that the tablet on social service would have to be re-chiseled to accommodate the forward thinking of that committee.

The cliché of "over-committeed and under-committed" was thrown in for what it was worth. Not much.

A strong suggestion was made and accepted that plans be designed so that those involved in social service programs would have an opportunity to reflect back with others on how the spirit had operated within their groups.

The unquenchable Pub idea came up again. The women suggested that they be included even though it is common knowledge that libation is available to them during the day at home.

The idea was tabled and will undoubtedly come up again at a later date.

In a thinly veiled attempt to get help, Elder Donoho suggested secondary assignments for elders so each area would have back-up support.

No one volunteered to back-up or support stewardship.

Since no one would help raise money—the next obvious subject of discussion was MEMBERSHIP.

Elder Barb Ellenberger got all kinds of good suggestions from her helpful associates:

1. Birddogging potential prospects to get them involved. One or two couples would take on the responsibility.
2. Getting them into a social shot after their worship experience.
3. Continuing to place main congregational thrust on new members.
4. Ruining the dynamic of the Ellenberger small group by including new people.
5. Letting one small group discuss the whole membership mess for a couple of months.
6. Sunday morning 4th group for new members to learn and St. Lukers to witness.

At this point the preaching minister gave some more lip service to democracy but insisted that Elder George Klein report on Children's Christian Education.

He reported himself as a leading contender for that kind of education, but said that Steve and the group had been doing swimmingly.

Dave Heegaard moved that the property area become a key benevolence project because of all the problems he faces.

The session offered the help of the Boy Scouts and the Ad-Hoc Standing Committee on Manse Refurbishing will be re-activated (and of course added to the management plan tablets).

Elder Ho talked more about stewardship and indicated the cash flow problem continues. Suggestions were made for alleviation.

Plans for One Great Hour of Sharing were discussed.

In a final flurry of activity before Hud's bedtime, the session approved letters of transfer for Fran and Bob Longley to Whitefish Bay, Wisconsin. It also approved transfers for the Vance Goodfellows to the Wayzata Community Church.

Barb Ellenberger is the next hostess on March 21.

The meeting was closed with a knockout prayer by Steve.

Dave Bell

Clerk of Session

3
THE CONSULTATION ON CHURCH UNION (COCU)

COCU Has No Sinew

There is much to be said for the tentative plan of church union.[1] For one thing, it is obvious that something must be done. The church just is not making it as it is presently structured. This is certainly the boldest approach to restructuring that has yet been devised.

For another thing, the plan is the best answer yet to the appalling provincialism that has beset the church for so long. The parish plan forces the church from its golden and not-so-golden ghettos to deal with the wounds of the world.

For a third thing, the emphasis upon "mission," while decades late, is forcefully made. The necessity for social action is recognized. Such an emphasis is timely and crucial.

In the fourth place, there is an historical aptness to the plan. It culminates 50 years of ecumenical efforts, which saw the creation of the National and World Councils of Churches and other agencies to begin to do together what could not be done alone. It is also, conceivably, one more step toward world union with the Catholics.

In the fifth place, the plan has a largeness of spirit which is encouraging. It affirms a continual reformation, even of the structure which it is suggesting. It spells out the right of nonconformity, the right of all to be fairly represented. Two children, for instance, as well as two young persons, are to be official participants in the service of inauguration.

But are all these things enough? In my opinion they are not. The plan is a good beginning, but it does not, in my opinion, go nearly far enough.

I

For one thing, there is the usual vagueness of such reports. It is not clear whether bishops are elected by regions (p. 64, pt. 60) or by districts (65.71). It is not clear whether district delegates are elected by parish councils (61.63) or by parishes (63.54). Nor is it clear what deacons are expected to do. Nor is it clear whether an ordained nonclergyman can be a bishop. Nor is it clear why some people should be ordained and some not.

II

More fundamental, it is not at all clear why structural union should be *the* goal of the church at this time. It is assumed rather than explained. Only seven paragraphs are devoted to the most essential element in any planning process, namely strategic or overall planning, which asks the question, What do we want to be? or the question, What do we want to do?

It could be argued, for instance, as I have suggested, that the *goal* of the church in the modern era is to be a suffering servant, the way its founder was. Indeed, such a goal is hinted in numerous places throughout the plan. Union may or may not be a *means* of reaching that goal.

Many would argue that union is *not* a means of achieving *that* end. Why? (1) Because union inevitably overemphasizes structure and underemphasizes mission. (2) Because for union to work you have to get so much compromise that you end up watering the church down rather than beefing it up. The bishops, for instance, are going to be too weak for Methodists and too strong for Presbyterians. An Episcopalian-type service in a parish will be fine for Episcopalians, excruciating for United Church members. And so on. (3) Because union will require enormous amounts of energy in the next few years which could better be expended in getting on with the church's mission, that of being a suffering servant. It is even possible that if the church does not get on with its mission now, there will be little church left to enjoy the luxury of union in 1980.

III

There is another fundamental vagueness. The *job* of the church member is *never* spelled out. It is only hinted in such words as "mission" and "service" and a section on "marks of membership" (23.6). The plan is so vague as to be virtually silent about what is *expected* of church members. There are *no* requirements. There is *no* job description. There is *no* discipline. There is *no* contract. A new church without such minimal standards as studying, sharing, and serving, which we have seen were the early church's own *kerygma, koinonia,* and *diakonia,* is no better than what we already have, namely a church without minimal standards which just simply is not cutting it with millions of starving people.

Jesus never backed off such standards. Take the rich man who came to him and wanted to join up. He had everything going for him, as most of the 25 million contemplating church union have, being American and middle-class. "Sell what you have and give to the poor," Jesus told him. The man wouldn't do it. So he didn't join. The standard of membership was sacrificial giving. There is *nothing* in the plan for church union about sacrificial giving. There is *nothing* in the plan for church union about any standard of church membership whatever.

Can you imagine any of those 25 million people taking a job in which there were no standards, no requirements, no contract, no job description?

If the *goal* of the church is suffering service the *means* for reaching the goal *must* be spelled out to the people who will be joining the church. There is *nothing* in the plan which spells out *anything* about what is *expected* of you if you are a church member. This is not only poor management. It is poor Bible.

IV

Not only is the plan vague about several minor items and two absolutely fundamental ones. It also fails to make clear (1) why votes must be conducted separately by separate houses of lay and ordained precisely when the point of union was to overcome separateness; (2) why its own committee fails from the very first in the principle of equitable representation, the one young member, to the best of my knowledge, being 25, there being only a handful of women, and no poor; (3) why there must be two nominees officially nominated for the national assembly when only one is so nominated for the parish, district, and region; (4) why the name of the church, The Church of Christ Uniting, is so utterly devoid of imagination; (5) why the old language of "mission," "ministry," "shepherd," "flock," and "fellowship," which just simply does not communicate to the young, the poor, the black, the labor leader is employed throughout; (6) why the old language is duplicated by old thinking: there is virtually nothing new about worship, the Bible, church membership, ministry, beau-reaucracy; the *only* thing new is the parish plan, and that is not really new, it is recent: many parishes are operating that way already.

V

Still another objection is the antihistorical nature of the plan. It could be argued that it is behind the times rather than with. It is, for instance, a time of black separatism. It is utterly illusory to think that the aggressive black leadership developing over the last few years will be the slightest bit interested in joining with whites in a 25-million-member church.

Furthermore, an historian might well tell us that the last half of the century is a time for pluralism, which is the antithesis of structural union. Look at the third and fourth party movements. Look at the youth culture in Consciousness III in the "Greening of America." Look at the breakup—I do not say breakdown—of values in everything from hair-styles to selective conscientious objection.

In light of these events, it could be argued that the church is as united as it can be or should be, that juridical union is neither timely nor helpful, that there are plenty of ways to show oneness in diversity and that the time has come to pursue the diversity rather than the oneness—particularly in view of the fact that there is a real danger that the pursuit of unity will drag everyone toward the middle and prevent precisely those creative church structures that are now evolving locally across the nation to meet the agony of our time.

VI

A sixth objection is that the plan of union has not, to my knowledge, been scrutinized by a management consultant firm. No firm worth its salt would have permitted such vagueness about goal or such traditionalism about means. The nine churches, in my opinion, should *pay* to have this plan assessed by the top three management consultant firms in the nation. They should also, in my opinion, *pay* to have it analyzed by the top three community organizers in the country. The loving references to social action would then become, overnight, immediate, specific, realizable, and actionable.

VII

However, all these objections pale beside the one fundamental objection—namely, that the entire plan, if we are going to plan in this way, has no muscle. Not only are there no job descriptions for the members, there are no *powers* for the judicatories. A judicatory is a decision-making body, and there are four of them in this plan of union: the parish council, the district, the region, and the national assembly. In none of them is the power to legislate, the power to execute, or the power to interpret spelled out. Such powers do not make a body top-heavy and overcentralized. They simply give it enough muscle to hold it up. This plan does not. Therefore you simply have another laissez-faire denomination, only bigger, and there is no reason whatever to expend valuable energy on that.

Now, to be sure, there is a feint in the direction of protecting this Achilles' heel. But it is only a feint. It does not come off. "The district," we read, and it is the same for the region and nation, "shall have power to . . ." (64.59). But to do what? "Nominate persons to the office of bishop." "Authorize the installation of presbyters and deacons." "Receive and transfer presbyters and deacons." Nothing new, nothing exciting, nothing for meeting the wounds of the world.

There are, however, three possibilities out of ten to show the muscle needed to make the plan attractive. The district has the power to "organize, realign, and dissolve parishes and district task groups." Fine. But nearly every denomination contemplating merger *already* has that power. It is rarely used and when used, used anemically. Proof is the surfeit of churches we have in this country, each allowed to go its merry way so long as Uncle Ezra pays the mortgage. Higher judicatories just simply will not move on lower judicatories unless their backs are against the wall. The entire church is structured bottom-up when it should be far more top-down. There is *no* top-down muscle spelled out in this plan of union. Therefore there is *no* reason why the united church should be any more adept at organizing, realigning and dissolving parishes than the divided church.

Another opportunity for muscle is that the district "adopts a budget for the district work." But that is *all* that is said. Nothing about levies. Nothing about taxes. Nothing about how much the parishes are going to be *assessed* to make the district work. We can only conclude that districts will accept whatever leftovers are given them by the parishes, which is precisely the way the church without muscle is operating now.

The final opportunity for muscle at all three levels is the fine clause, "review and redirect the work of parishes and district task groups." Again, virtually all the denominations contemplating merger have that power now. The point is they do not use it, and the point is they will not use it unless it is *spelled out* that they are *expected* to use it, that they have the *power* to legislate, the *power* to execute, the *power* to interpret; that their decisions are *binding* on the lower judicatory; and that if the lower judicatory does not like it, it can *appeal*.

Again, it is the federal question, and it goes all the way back to Hamilton and Madison and Jefferson. They resolved it then, and there is no reason why the plan of union cannot resolve it now. Build in the federal principle, and the plan would have much to commend itself. Without it, we are no better off than we were. As a matter of fact we are worse off, because our energy is drained in a fruitless endeavor as we are inexorably dragged toward the middle and away from our creative thrusts.

As a beginning, the plan of union should set standards of membership for the new church and then *spell out* the powers of the national assembly, including the power to "set fiscal standards," and work its way *down* to the powers of the local parish, which, in the plan of union, is as omnipotent and balkanized as it has ever been, thanks to that good old laissez-faire sop, "the parish will be responsible for its own life and work" (59.26).

The Consultation has a unique opportunity to do a new thing. I hope it will.

Notes

CHAPTER 3. HOW TO WRITE A PLAN FOR YOUR CHURCH

1. Published by Union College Character Research Project, 10 Nott Terrace, Schenectady, New York 12308.
2. Retreats.

CHAPTER 4. THE CHURCH AS SUFFERING SERVANT

1. O. Cullmann in G. Kittel, *Theological Dictionary of the New Testament* (Ann Arbor, Mich.: Eerdmans, 1968), vol. 6, p. 110.
2. G. Johnston in *The Interpreter's Dictionary of the Bible* (Nashville: Abingdon, 1962), vol. 3, p. 169.
3. A. Richardson in G. Johnston, *op. cit.,* vol. 4, p. 179.
4. G. Lampe in G. Johnston, *op. cit.,* vol. 2, p. 627.
5. E. Hamlin in G. Johnston, *op. cit.,* vol. 3, p. 519.

CHAPTER 6. THE CHURCH SHARES

1. F. Hauck in G. Kittel, *Theological Dictionary of the New Testament* (Grand Rapids, Mich.: Eerdmans, 1965), vol. 3, p. 797.

184

2. James Muilenburg in *The Interpreter's Dictionary of the Bible* (Nashville: Abingdon, 1962), vol. 2, p. 617.
3. Hauck, *op. cit.,* p. 806.
4. R. T. Stamm in *The Interpreter's Bible* (Nashville: Abingdon, 1953), vol. 10, p. 578.
5. Rom. 1: 7; 1 Cor. 4:14; Phil. 2:12; 2 Pet. 3:14 *et pas.*

CHAPTER 7. THE CHURCH SERVES

1. H. Beyer in G. Kittel, *Theological Dictionary of the New Testament,* (Ann Arbor, Mich.: Eerdmans, 1964), vol. 2, p. 84.
2. *Idem.*
3. *Idem.*
4. E. Stauffer in G. Kittel, *op. cit.,* vol. 1, p. 44 (ital. add.).
5. *Ibid.,* p. 46.
6. *Minneapolis Tribune,* March 16, 1969.
7. *1970 New York Times Almanac,* p. 304.
8. *Ibid.,* p. 301.
9. Minneapolis *Tribune,* editorial, February 10, 1971.
10. *Idem.*
11. *1970 New York Times Almanac,* p. 302.
12. Richard Parker, *Center Magazine,* March, 1970.
13. *Minneapolis Star,* April 9, 1970.
14. Parker, *op. cit.*
15. Robert L. Heilbroner, "Benign Neglect in the United States," *Trans-Action,* October, 1970.
16. Hal Cohen and Arthur Miller, Nationwide 1968 *Study,* Institute for Social Research, University of Michigan.
17. *Minneapolis Tribune,* June 25, 1970.
18. Thomas Jefferson, *First Inaugural Address.*
19. Thomas Fleming, quoted in *Reader's Digest,* July, 1969.

CHAPTER 15. HOW TO BE ORGANIZED BY THE SPIRIT

1. Quoted by Roger Hazelton in *The Christian Century,* January 20, 1965.
2. E. Schweizer in G. Kittel, *Theological Dictionary of the New Testament*

(Grand Rapids, Mich.: Eerdmans, 1968), vol. 6, p. 424.
3. Quoted in *New York Times Magazine,* April 16, 1972.
4. *Minneapolis Star,* October 14, 1971.

APPENDIX 3

1. The plan is available from the National Council of Churches, 475 Riverside Drive, New York City, N. Y. 10027.

73 74 75 76 77 10 9 8 7 6 5 4 3 2 1